"Alvin Reid stands apart among educators as a high-energy, proactive, and experienced leader in the field of youth ministry. In *As You Go*, he casts a powerful light on the way forward and helps us see that youth ministry has a purposeful role in God's mission to restore His glory. You will be highly engaged while you read this book and greatly motivated when you put it down! That's just what we need in youth ministry today."

—ROGER GLIDEWELL, president, Global Youth Ministry

"Dr. Reid challenges the youth pastor, volunteer, pastor, parent, and teen to take a look at how they are leading and to live missionally according to Scripture. Everyone needs to pick up this book and read it. I pray this book speaks into the lives of many youth pastors and leaders and challenges all of us to lead as we go."

—BRIAN MILLS, youth pastor, Long Hollow Baptist Church, Henderson, Tennessee; coauthor of *Checkpoints*

"In *As You Go*, Alvin Reid brings much-needed dialogue to the conversation about creating students who are true disciples moving from great consumers to Great Commissioners. I, like Dr. Reid, believe that it begins and ends with the gospel."

—J. ROGER DAVIS, president, Student Life

"Alvin Reid gets it! Those are the exact words I kept saying to my wife as I read this book while sitting next to her on the plane. Reid understands that to have effective biblical student ministries, one must have a firm grasp on theology and methodology. He has crafted a model that can and should be implemented in student ministries globally."

—MIKE CALHOUN, executive assistant to the president, Word of Life Fellowship; author of *Where Was God When . . . ?*

"Dr. Alvin Reid is a flaming ball of ministry phenomenon. He inspires with his winsome southern charm yet informs with a heart and intellect that beat for a coming kingdom. The marvel of this book is its profundity in a conversational tone. I'm confident *As You Go* will be a catalyst for the next great awakening, which—up until this work—student leaders and parents have only dreamed about."

—TONY NOLAN, Tony Nolan Ministries; speaker and author

"What student ministry needs is what this book proposes. This is a return to a first-century imperative with a twenty-first–century practice. It will be required reading for our staff!"

—MATT LAWSON, high school pastor,
First Baptist Woodstock, Woodstock, Georgia; author of *TWISDOM*

"The resurgence of a generation desiring to exist for more than simply the American dream is rising. *As You Go* is a must-read for all those in the trenches of student ministry. It should be highly considered as a shaping tool defining and clarifying the direction of your ministry toward keeping the gospel the resounding anthem!"

—ED NEWTON, Bible communicator

"Alvin Reid not only understands student ministry, he loves students! His passion to see teenagers discipled and growing in the gospel is evident in *As You Go*. This book will be an asset for your ministry as you lead students to be more like Jesus."

—JEFF BORTON, coauthor of *Simple Student Ministry*;
pastor of students, Christ Fellowship, Miami

"I've been one of those voices calling teenagers to total-life purity, but getting teenagers through high school without babies is not the ultimate goal. I've been one of those voices calling youth ministry in the direction of the family, but families holding hands and singing 'Kumbaya' in the den is not the ultimate goal. Getting the whole gospel to the whole world is the ultimate goal, and Alvin Reid proudly proclaims that missional youth groups are central to that goal. Not only that, Reid nails the process required."

—RICHARD ROSS, PhD, professor of student ministry,
Southwestern Baptist Theological Seminary

"Alvin Reid makes a unique contribution. He calls for the blending of missional ecclesiology and Christ-centered identity in order to release a wave of well-discipled students who love the church and are dialed into God's mission. Pastors and parents should read this book and collaborate for a future generation of diverse, culture-renewing, Christ-proclaiming missionaries who turn the world upside down. I look forward to implementing these insights and watching the Spirit move through the next generation."

—JONATHAN DODSON, founding pastor, Austin City Life Church;
author of *Gospel-Centered Discipleship* and *Unbelievable Gospel*

# ALVIN L. REID

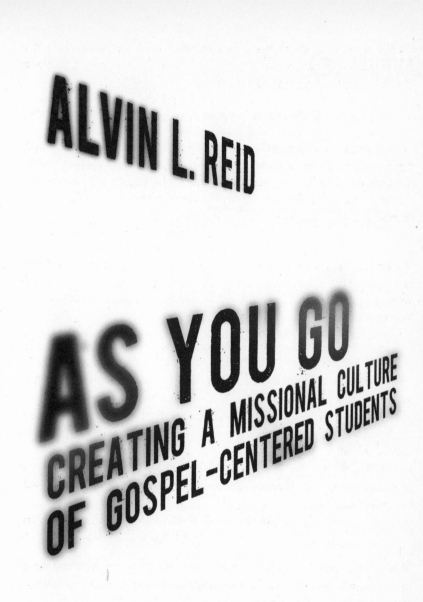

# AS YOU GO

## CREATING A MISSIONAL CULTURE OF GOSPEL-CENTERED STUDENTS

TH1NK

TH1NK, an
Imprint of
NavPress

NavPress is the publishing ministry of The Navigators, an international Christian organization and leader in personal spiritual development. NavPress is committed to helping people grow spiritually and enjoy lives of meaning and hope through personal and group resources that are biblically rooted, culturally relevant, and highly practical.

**For a free catalog go to www.NavPress.com or call 1.800.366.7788 in the United States or 1.800.839.4769 in Canada.**

NavPress titles may be purchased in bulk for ministry, educational, business, fund-raising, or sales promotional use. For information, please call NavPress Special Markets at 1.800.504.2924.

ISBN-13: 978-1-61291-302-5

Cover design by Arvid Wallen

Reid, Alvin L.
    As you go : creating a missional culture of gospel-centered students / Alvin Reid.
        pages cm
    Includes bibliographical references.
    ISBN 978-1-61291-302-5
    1. Missions—Theory. 2. Discipling (Christianity)  I. Title.
    BV2063.R435 2013
    266.001—dc23
                            2012036645

Printed in the United States of America

2 3 4 5 6 7 8 / 18 17 16 15 14 13

*To Michelle:*

*my bride of over thirty years*

*and the mother of our two Millennial children,*

*Josh and Hannah.*

*I love you.*

# CONTENTS

# FOREWORD

As Alvin notes in this book, student ministry has undergone several metamorphoses in the last few years. Out of a concern that we might "lose" the next generation, we gave ourselves to gimmicks that eventually did nothing but dampen the next generation's awareness of the distinctive power of the gospel. Others, often in reaction to such silliness, suggested that student ministry no longer had any value for the church, and perhaps never did. Alvin shows us, however, that student ministry presents some truly unique opportunities and that the gospel itself contains all the power necessary for it.

Here are a few reasons I love *As You Go* and think it will transform the discussion around student ministry:

This book is centered on the gospel. Alvin understands that the gospel is not simply the diving board off of which we jump into the pool of Christianity; it is the pool itself. He contends that a generation will go no farther for God in the world than they have gone deep in the gospel.

This book recognizes that you cannot separate gospel and mission, because only accurate gospel theology produces effective missiology. "Missions" is not something done by one department in the church; it is the very nature of Christian discipleship.

This book sets the context of ministry in the secular sphere. Of the forty miracles recorded in the book of Acts, thirty-nine happened outside the church walls. That means our theater for ministry must be the community. If the gospel does not transform the home, school, and extracurricular lives of students, it will have no relevance. Our success therefore cannot be measured merely by how many students we gather, but also by how effectively we empower them. Sending capacity is as crucial a mark of success as seating capacity.

This book is local-church-centered. The local church is an institution that Jesus shed His blood to establish. While not ignoring the significant contributions of parachurch ministries or minimizing their ongoing contribution, this book urges a return to the local church as the locus of New Testament ministry.

This book is both culturally savvy and biblically mature. Alvin's winsome style sometimes masks the fastidiousness of his scholarship and the clarity of his insight. But make no mistake: This is not a book by a backwoods preacher postulating on how things "ought to be." This is a reasoned, researched analysis of where we are, how we got here, and where we need to go.

This book takes a younger generation seriously. Some of the most significant recent movements in our world have been led by young men and women under the age of twenty. The multibillion-dollar Facebook, arguably the greatest business phenomenon of our generation, was started by a nineteen-year-old. With 52 percent of the world's population now under the age of thirty, should we not be holding up in front of this generation a vision of what *God* wants for the world?

As a personal friend and mentee of Alvin's, I can tell you that he practices what he preaches. Hardly ever am I with the man when he is not sharing Christ with someone or telling me about someone he is discipling. He is a never-ending source of firsthand stories of God's work in the lives of people around him.

Alvin took me aside when I was a student, believed in me, and invested in me. He told me that his greatest ministry joy was seeing students, like me, achieve all that God had for us. John Calvin once said the ability to call out and raise up leaders was among those gifts to be held in highest regard in the church. If that is the case, then Alvin is one of the finest Christian leaders I have ever known.

Alvin has never let me forget that Jesus came to seek and save the lost, nor that those of us who follow Him must do the same. His passion for the salvation of students oozes out of these pages. It is contagious.

My prayer is that Alvin's book will catalyze a return to the biblical model of student ministry: gospel-rich, church-centered, family-based, mission-compelling discipleship. Might we be on the eve of the next great awakening in our country, and might this book represent God's movement in the generation of students who will lead it?

J. D. GREEAR
lead pastor, the Summit Church, Durham, North Carolina;
author of *Gospel: Recovering the Power That Made Christianity Revolutionary*

# ACKNOWLEDGMENTS

First of all, I want to thank the Author and Finisher of our faith, my Lord and Savior Jesus Christ. The older I get, the more I learn just how great His grace is. The gospel is the greatest message we could ever know, follow, live, and share.

I want to thank my family: Michelle, my wife of more than thirty years. You have put up with so much: my traveling, my ADD, and my writing, to name just a few things, and you have been the perfect example of a godly mom to our children. Josh and Hannah, you have taught me more than I have ever taught you. By the time this book is released, you will both be married. God has taken you on a phenomenal journey so far, and your mom and I are excited to see what He does in the coming days.

I want to thank students who read chapters or more of the manuscript to help me think well about the subject. In particular, these included doctoral students Jason Mitchell, Susan Booth, Josh Laxton, Jeremy Couture, Dave Miller, Greg Hauss, and Cameron Wooten. I want to thank a group of student pastors who read the manuscript near its completion and gave insights from the front lines: Mike Camire, Joon Park, Joey Rolen, Russell Whitefield, and Michael Wood, as well as Lilli Mitchell, a student pastor's wife. My colleagues who help me in teaching student ministry at Southeastern Baptist Theological Seminary, including our visiting professor of student ministry, Jimmy Scroggins, and my coteacher in our missional student ministry class, Jeff Lovingood, have taught me a great deal about ministry to students in recent days.

Peggy Loafman, the world-famous faculty secretary in the west wing of Jacumin-Simmons (the wing of cool), has been tireless in her help on this and many other projects. Thanks, Peggy, for your help. I particularly want to thank my president, my boss, and my friend, Danny Akin, along with Dean Ken Keathley and the board of trustees for kindly granting me a half sabbatical to finish the writing of this book. George Robinson has become one of my best friends on earth in addition to serving as a colleague. Thank you, George, for your love to me. Bruce Ashford, dean of our college, came up with the idea of my focusing on student ministry at Southeastern as well as my interest in evangelism. That was a move of great insight, and I thank you, Bruce, for it. All my colleagues at Southeastern, the greatest seminary ever, have shaped me in some way.

This is my first book with NavPress, though I hope not my last. Thank you, longtime friends Michael Miller and Barry Sneed along with Marsha Pursley (the queen of marketing) and so many others. I am honored to be part of the team.

And then there is that great host of student pastors who bless me constantly. I am sure I will leave out many, but these in particular have encouraged me on this journey: Matt Lawson, Jeff Borton, Kelly Knouse, Brian Mills, Nate Dooley, Brian Smith, Dan Elkins, Jason Gaston, Jeff Stockdale, Brent Crowe, Justin Buchanan, Jay Strack, and John Mark Harrison.

While so many have influenced me, this work is mine, in particular the shortcomings.

# INTRODUCTION

On the east coast of North Carolina, the state I call home, a windy spot named Kitty Hawk faces the Atlantic Ocean. On that site some one hundred years ago, two brothers named Orville and Wilbur Wright made a discovery that has radically changed my life and most likely yours as well. On a cold December day in 1903, these brothers tested what became the first fixed-wing flying machine in history. Their efforts marked the tipping point of a movement leading to global air travel, which has become a staple of culture now. A century later, in Atlanta alone, numbers equivalent to a small city pass through a single airport, traveling literally all over the world in a matter of hours.

Airplanes have not changed travel in its essence — the movement of people from one geographical location to another. But the means and speed of travel have changed dramatically.

We have an unchanging Word from God (the Bible) and a unique message (the gospel), but the world in which we teach and live and share the truth of a relationship with God has changed significantly in recent years:

- Fifty-two percent of the world's population is under thirty.[1]
- In the United States more youth walk our streets, ride in school buses, and fill our malls than ever in our country's history.

The Millennials (those born between roughly 1978 and 2000) number 95 million, far more than their 78 million Boomer parents.[2]

- The Millennial generation is the most studied and in some ways most unique generation in the history of the West.
- A flattened world shaped by the Internet and immediacy has created a renaissance in youth culture.

Student ministry in churches must recognize the new world in which we live and change—not the message but the approach—for this new world.

From the earliest days of the church in Acts until now, the Great Commission has not changed in its essence. But the approach to the missionary enterprise of taking the gospel to the world has changed dramatically. Peter and Paul had ink to pen their writings, but no blogs or Twitter feeds. Those of us who live in the West and in particular the United States must recognize the nature of the world we live in, the world which is the mission field we pray for and send missionaries to.

The United States has become the fourth-largest mission field in the world; though this is a sobering reality, it also provides unique opportunities we'll explore. Across our nation, in most (if not all) of the following contexts, you will find more people who do not follow Christ than people who do:

- Public schools and universities
- Businesses
- Subdivisions and apartment buildings
- Government offices
- Hospitals
- Prisons

In virtually every place not explicitly deemed "Christian," like a church or Christian school, you are almost guaranteed to find more who think they do not need Christ than people who walk with Him. We live in a mission field. Children grow up in a place of great need for the gospel. For many of us who walk with Christ and in particular involve ourselves with students, this means a fundamental shift must take place:

- Pastors must continue to teach the Word but also see themselves increasingly as missionary strategists helping to shepherd their flock to think and live as missionaries. This includes student pastors.
- Church planting must continue to have a high profile, especially in the major cities.
- Families must take a more intentional role in the missional preparation of their own children.
- Student ministers must recognize more students today are lost without Christ than ever in history, and the "market share" of students active in church is shrinking.

## IN OTHER WORDS, STUDENT MINISTRY NEEDS A REVOLUTION

What I write about in these pages serves as a student-focused aspect of a much larger conversation going on in the church today. We live in a time when much is at stake and much is changing. The gospel does not change, but we live in a time as revolutionary as the Renaissance and Reformation, a time when the stakes will not allow status quo Christianity to continue unchallenged, if any season ever did. Unrest does not equal change, but it does offer an opportunity for change.

In the fall of 2011, I listened with interest to one of the founders of what is probably the largest, most influential student ministry organization in my lifetime make a startling confession regarding a generation of youth ministry. Wayne Rice, of Youth Specialties, observed, "We got what we wanted. We turned youth ministry into the toy department of the church. Churches now hire professionals to lead youth ministry. We got relevance but we created a generation of teenagers who are a mile wide and are an inch deep."

That, my friends, is a remarkable confession. Student ministries and churches in general have not equipped students to be adults who understand the gospel and live as missionaries. We created a "cool" subculture where students could be treated like the center of the universe and given a bunch of stuff, but not enough Jesus.

I am tired of meeting young adults who tell me that what they remember from their youth group experience is "Invite a friend" and "Don't have sex." This book is not intended to focus on what is wrong in student ministry, however, but to offer a new (or renewed) way of thinking.

To his credit, Wayne Rice then argued for three changes. First, turn student ministry back over to the church. Youth pastors should be seeking to work themselves out of a job, he argued, as they help youth become incorporated into the life of the church. Second, we can no longer ignore the role of the parents. Third, we can offer them nothing better than the gospel.

The following pages will offer a way of thinking about teenagers for student pastors, churches, parents, and students themselves. We need a return to a radically Christ-centered focus.

## SO HOW DO WE GET (BACK) TO GOSPEL-CENTERED STUDENT MINISTRY?

First, **God**. We need a new vision of God: His vastness, His involvement in everything, His power, His love and justice. If your students have a lot better grasp of who you are as the student pastor than who God is as the mighty Creator of the universe who sustains the world by the power of His Word, you have a problem. If your students understand the latest stats on sexuality in America more than they know the attributes of God and how He is King over all of life, you have a serious problem. We need student pastors and national and parachurch leaders who are better at theology than at new ideas. Rice noted that the founders of Young Life said that it is a sin to make Christianity boring. Agreed. And it is a greater sin to make Christianity silly, which is what has happened far too often. We must exalt a great God and give focus to His Word.

Second, the **gospel**. The next thing you should read is not a book on youth ministry. Read the Gospels and the book of Romans. Then read *Gospel* by J. D. Greear or *The Gospel for Real Life* by Jerry Bridges. We have taken the good news of the gospel off the headlines of our ministries where it should always be, and we have put it in the advice column part of our youth groups. We pull the gospel out to give advice rather than showing students how Jesus is the hero of all of Scripture, all of life, all the parts of their lives, and showing them how the gospel makes sense of everything. Let me remind you that in newspapers, advice columns are next to the cartoons. And that is what we do with the gospel, putting it next to an iPad giveaway instead of always show-casing it as the main event, the one thing that is constantly newsworthy in your ministry. We need a radical, Christocentric transformation, understanding the gospel is for salvation and sanctification, for saved and unsaved alike. Jesus is the answer to all of life—not the thin, superficial, subcultural Jesus, but the Jesus who cares for the broken and rebukes the self-righteous—the children-loving, disciple-calling, leper-healing, Pharisee-rebuking, humbly born, and ultimately reigning Lord Jesus.

Third, the **goal**. Ultimately the goal of any ministry is to glorify God. I submit the goal of student ministry is to glorify God by develop-ing disciples who learn both to see the world as missionaries and live as missionaries—to live focused on the mission of God. The goal is not to have a great event with a lot of buzz. This means we will do less student ministry that is based on the lowest common denominator, a term I will mention often. It means you score success in long-term discipleship, equipping students for a life of service to Christ. It means helping students grow and develop their own plan for gospel impact now. If you help individual students develop a plan for gospel advance in the context of your local church, you will in fact help them hear from God and be confident in their planning, and thus be better prepared for college and life.

Fourth, the **gathering**. Connect to the whole church, across generations. Today's generation of teens is not only the largest ever, it is also the most fatherless. We must connect students to the larger church and not function as a parachurch ministry within a church building. Students need older believers in their lives. We need a Titus 2 revolution where older men teach younger guys and older women teach younger ladies.

I am not trying to offer in these pages a "how to do student ministry" book, although I hope you will find it to be of practical help. We have spent so much time on the imperative that I fear we have lost the indicative, the "why" of all we do with, for, and through students. What I am trying to do is argue that every student ministry—in fact every local church, parachurch ministry, and for that matter every Christian family and individual—has a posture, a perspective from which we seek to live. And the current posture of student ministry could be greatly corrected. I suppose I am offering an orthopedic or chiropractic corrective to help those who love students—parents, pastors, student pastors, student workers—and students themselves understand the core focus of life. If we get that right, we can figure out the how-to a lot more easily. But if we fail here, no cool student building or hipster youth guy can help.

I simply argue that once a person meets Christ he or she goes on a journey to further understand the message of God and live out the mission of God, to build a gospel-centered life with a missional posture toward everything: career, family, church, economics, fitness, morality—*everything*.

Gabe Lyons, in *The Next Christians*, observes via research what I see consistently in my frequent interactions with leaders: Leaders who seek a "new way forward," who want Christianity to mean something much more akin to our roots, who "want to be a force for restoration in a broken world even as we proclaim the Christian Gospel."[3] I, and others, call this way forward *missional*. Being missional means to think like a missionary, and missionaries travel: geographically to far lands, or sometimes they simply take a journey into their own communities to share Christ more effectively and intentionally. Geography does not define a missionary; the mission does. But to serve as a reminder that whatever a student's vocation or location, as a Christ follower he or she is a missionary, each chapter will begin with a place on the globe, for at every place mentioned there are people who were created to worship and who need to see His great love. Including your own neighborhood.

The title chosen for this book comes from a significant nuance in the language of the Great Commission. Jesus' final words in the gospel of Matthew are often summarized: "Go therefore and make disciples of all nations." Without getting overly technical, the only command in the Great Commission is *make disciples*. Everything else explains the imperative mission of making disciples. The word translated *go* has a unique tense and mood in the Greek (aorist participle) that can be understood as a timeless description of action. The Great Commission is not: *Go someday*. It is: *Going* and *having gone*, make disciples, *as you go*.

Creating a missional culture of gospel-centered students requires you to be making disciples *as you go*. It is a lifestyle. It is a movement. It won't happen overnight. So wherever you are today, make disciples. Wherever you are going tomorrow, make disciples. Having gone into your neighborhood and to the ends of the earth, make disciples. The people of every nation need the gospel.

I am finishing this book in Kiev, Ukraine, on a mission trip. But the mission here is the same as the mission in my neighborhood. Life is a mission trip: Take it. Let's go on the journey together. I pray we will take a whole generation with us.

# CHAPTER 1

# MISSIONAL GENERATION

## *Johannesburg, South Africa*

One of the great global cities of our time, Joburg was the initial stop on my first trip to the great continent of Africa. I also began a relationship with a group of people who hold a special place in my heart to this day, but I don't mean the students who joined me or the new believers we met.

I am referring to the TSA, or Transportation Security Administration.

If you travel by air, you know the dear people who have the joy of screening passengers at airports across the United States and their peers in airports globally. Because I have the joy of an artificial hip (insert sarcastic tone), I have the privilege of knowing TSA personnel up close and personal.

"Step to the side, sir. Male assist!" Have you ever heard that? If you have ever heard the familiar beeping of a metal detector you just set off in an airport (and you are a male), you have. I have flown all over the world multiple times and have set off more metal detectors than I can recall. I know the airport security drill.

The drill changes through the years. I remember when you could greet your loved ones at the gate. The details change over time, but what remains constant is this: If you set off the metal detector, you will have to be screened further. Maybe you forgot the change in your pocket or failed to take off your belt. If you have set it off, you know what happens next: The personal screener gets a little more than intrusive to make sure you are safe to travel. Today, most airports have magnetic resonance machines that allow me to avoid the "personal touch" of such thorough customer care. And why do I have that infernal artificial hip? Why? Because of the hazards of student ministry.

I broke my hip at a youth camp in 1996. My team won the mud volleyball game, I won the trash talking, but I lost the ensuing wrestling match. Two years later, after a lot of pain and misdiagnosis by doctors (there is a reason they call it *practicing* medicine), I received an artificial hip. That alone will ruin your whole day. I was thirty-eight years old, still fairly active athletically, and more than a little bummed that my wrestling days with our growing children were over. I now have a piece of titanium jammed in my femur, a joy that slows me down every time I fly.

I received my metal hip in 1998. But I started setting off metal detectors in 2001, in late September in fact, on the aforementioned trip to South Africa. Why did my hip suddenly begin to set off the metal detector? Three numbers: 9-1-1. The terrorist attack on the U.S. changed a lot of lives and at some level has touched the whole world. Why?

Several years before that September a man sitting in a tent in eastern Afghanistan had become pretty ticked off at the West and at Americans in particular. Osama bin Laden convinced a couple dozen men to come to the States to attend flight-training schools to learn how to fly domestic air carriers. These men boarded flights on September 11, 2001, and armed with nothing more than box cutters and the ability to steer airliners, unleashed an attack unprecedented in American history, leaving almost three thousand dead.

For students, the specter of terrorism would affect their generation the way the Cold War affected mine.

Immediately after the attacks, the metal detectors were turned to a more sensitive frequency. For the first time in three years of having a metal hip, I set off a metal detector less than two weeks after 9/11.

Osama bin Laden started a movement of the worst kind. He led a handful of men to conduct a most sinister act, one that has led to the recognition of a global movement of terrorism just when we thought the Cold War's end would lead to a much more peaceful world.

While many have been involved, one man started the movement.

He was not a dictator.

Nor was he the leader of a massive, organized army.

But using an idea and modern communication tools such as social media, Osama bin Laden has to some degree changed the whole world. Not for the better.

Good news: Almost two thousand years ago a band of believers, a gaggle of Galileans, a den of disciples numbering only 120, gathered in a big room in Jerusalem. They had no standing in the culture. But they had a mission so big only God could accomplish it through them. He took a man intent on leading a movement to persecute followers of Christ and turned him into one of the leaders of the early Christian movement. Saul of Tarsus became the apostle Paul because of the power of the gospel.

You are reading this book right now because these and others like them lived the mission given to us by our Lord.

Student ministry today stands at a crossroad. My purpose in this book is to show student pastors and parents, those who work with students and students themselves, what should be at the core of our ministries to students. And, in so doing, I hope to show what the entire Western church needs: a recovery of the gospel-centered, missional impulse seen in Acts and at other times in history, in particular times of great awakenings and missionary advance.

We need a vision for our youth bigger than any cultural indoctrination. We need a missional shift in students.

## WHY "MISSIONAL"?

Why the term *missional*? I use the term because students today, as a generation, stand ready for a challenge as big as life itself. Missional means to see the world with the eyes of a missionary, to look at everything and everyone from the posture of one on a mission so great that everything in life flows from that mission. Student ministry can play an integral role in helping the church meet the challenge of being missional. I respect those who have opted for a family-integrated model, or other approaches that essentially abolish student ministry as an ongoing part of the local church, but I believe student ministry needs reformation, not annihilation. I also believe the system currently in operation in many churches—more pizza parties than theological passion and more games than gospel—must be changed. The system is broken, and nothing less than a gospel infusion and cultural shift in the local church and in parachurch student ministries is needed. In the following chapters I will unpack essential features of effective student ministry for our time and for this generation.

## TURNING MILLENNIALS INTO MISSIONARIES

By "missional students," I mean simply this: The core of student ministry must be the mission of God, centered on knowing God and the living and loving and sharing of the gospel. Every student ministry—every local church group, every parachurch ministry, every book written about student ministry—has some idea of what the heart of student ministry should be. In practice it seems that too many focus on what I call the Big Three Es: events, entertainment, and externals (that is, behavior modification). This leads to other issues, like the personality-driven student ministry focused on the Pied Piper student pastor who himself is the main event.

I'm certainly not a hater of events; I speak at scores of them annually. Nor do I think a paintball tournament, especially as a means to build relationships, is a bad idea. The problem comes when many (perhaps most?) student ministries use *tools* like events or activities as the actual *template* for student ministry. The coming year of ministry starts with the big events—the Disciple Now (DNow) weekend, the camp, the mission trip—and then builds around them. That is event-driven student ministry. Missional student ministry starts with the posture of the student ministry as a missionary outpost in the community, utilizing tools like events and activities only as they assist in the fulfillment of the mission.

Talking with student pastors in churches with participation ranging from a handful of students to thousands reveals dissatisfaction with a version of student ministry that essentially strings together a series of events aimed at an adolescent-focused culture with a little discipleship thrown in. This is an overstatement, of course, and I hope not to paint too negative a picture. But it is the reality far more than we may want to admit. Student ministry should be about turning Millennials into missionaries, not helping church kids hang in there and have a good time.

> Missional: to see the world with the eyes of a missionary, to think like a missionary, and to relate to others as a missionary with a message of the gospel. In short, life is ministry. Make disciples as you go.

Like a rising tsunami, a missional shift swells before our very eyes in the Western church. Such a shift should not only involve student ministry but in no small way be led by it as well. Let me lay my cards on the table right here: I am not confident that my generation of baby boomers in the church will be successful in making the turn to a missional lifestyle. But I believe students today not only can but must make the shift. Read the pages of Scripture and you will see times when young adults played key roles in spiritual renewal and change. Study the life of Samuel, Josiah, and Esther, among others. Read how Paul exhorted

Timothy not only to refuse to allow older believers to look down on his youth but to set a living example instead. Read the stories of great spiritual movements and see how God used people from a young age in His great work: God began a hundred-year Moravian prayer revival out of twenty-seven-year-old Nikolaus von Zinzendorf's burden for youth. God began a movement of foreign missions in the United States under a haystack with a bunch of college students. He used a young Charles Spurgeon, barely out of his teens, to challenge London with the gospel. He used others like Jonathan Edwards, who challenged youth in his time and witnessed a Great Awakening. People today in their teens win gold medals at the Olympics and fight in wars. They can make an impact now in the church. But they need our help, our advocacy.

Reggie McNeal observes the need for the change happening in our time:

> All this calls for an expression of Christian spirituality that does not reflect or rely on the Constantinian world order for its major self-understanding. After Constantine, Christianity became a clergy-dominated religion centered around designated places of worship. This differed radically from its first three centuries. The movement founded by Jesus was largely a marketplace phenomenon, an organic connection among people who were experiencing a way of life together.[1]

## THE MISSIONAL SHIFT IN THE WESTERN CHURCH

From the church *plant* (facilities) to church *planting*

From *attractional* evangelism as the foundation to *incarnational* evangelism

From *maintaining institutions* to *advancing a movement*

From *compartmentalization* to *integration*

From *minimalistic gospel presentations* to *grand narrative conversations*

From *local* to *glocal (local to global)*

From *methodology-centered* to *gospel-centered*

From *events* to *process*

From *the lowest common denominator* to *self-feeders*

Let me unpack in a little more detail what I mean by developing missional students. Missional student ministry flows out of a missional church seeking to create missional students. The compartmentalization of student ministry from the life of the church, often functioning as a virtual parachurch ministry using the church facility, must be replaced with an integrated approach involving the whole church ministering to the whole body, with specific application to various groups such as students and senior adults. In 1 John 2 we read teachings addressed to "children," "young men," and "fathers." Focusing on a given group, such as students, can be validated in Scripture, but such focus should always grow out of the mission of God as applied in the local faith family.

## THE 411 ON THE MISSIONAL CHURCH

The Missional Church Network suggests three theological distinctives helpful to understanding what is meant by missional church, which I will apply to student ministry today.

First, **a missional church focuses on the missionary nature of God and His church.**[2] Our God is a sending God: The Father sent the Son, the Son sent the Spirit, and the Father, Son, and Spirit send the church. Likewise, student ministry should help students and their families see how their lives should grow out of the mission of God. The mission of God is more than a phrase—it summarizes the message of Scripture, indeed the message of Christianity. In chapter 2, I will explore further the gospel narrative of Creation, Fall, Rescue, and Restoration. Christopher Wright speaks eloquently of this narrative in his book *The Mission of God*. Wright argues that the whole counsel of God in Scripture is in its very nature missional, and that the hermeneutic, or the means by which we interpret all of Scripture, is mission.[3]

We were created in the image of God to worship Him alone. Because of the Fall, we worship the creation (often ourselves!) instead of God. Read Romans, all of it, and you will see this. As we center our ministries on the gospel, we rediscover the missionary God who seeks to save sinners. By missing the mission of God in all Scripture and for all of life, the church can easily become a provider of religious goods and services instead of "the gathered and sent people of God."[4]

A biblical focus means reading and teaching all Scripture with gospel lenses—preaching the gospel to believers and unbelievers. It means student leaders demonstrate a lifestyle of repentance and cultivate a culture of wonder at the gospel. It means creating a safe place for those who do not yet "get" the gospel (whether radically unchurched or steeped in/blinded by religion).

Being missional means to focus on the supernatural, Spirit-led work of God. Study the history of great spiritual movements and you will see young people involved throughout. Jonathan Edwards said the First Great Awakening—a remarkable revival in the 1700s that changed the American colonies and helped shape what would become the United States—was essentially a youth movement. What if this generation of students was set on fire by the Holy Spirit to see God work in power? This does not mean the end of events, but it does mean ministry that looks more like the mentoring focus of Jesus with His twelve, or that of Paul with Timothy, Titus, Silas, and many others in the New Testament. We learn spirituality best up close, not in an arena.

Developing missional students must be intentional: It involves creating a culture in which proclamation of the gospel is the center of both students' lives and church/student ministry. Missional does not mean learning to engage the culture while simultaneously failing to share the good news of Jesus with that culture. The result we long to see is for unbelievers to know and worship God.

We will not create missional students by merely implementing missional programming. Missional means helping students think, react, and live as missionaries in a broken and lost culture. Thus the focus of this book is to help you develop a student ministry culture, an ethos, in which students take the posture of missionaries, living to fulfill the mission of God through the gospel of God regardless of vocation or location.

Doing this will require a fundamental shift in our teaching. Much of what we do in student ministry focuses on the lowest common denominator: What truth can we teach that will apply to all? In an attractional, event-driven ministry, this approach is necessary to keep people coming. And, if your ministry focuses more on the how of Christianity (how to date better, how to witness, how to be happy) than on the why (focusing on God and His plan), it will thus be more focused on truth that applies to the widest possible audience. But the more we focus on helping students see the big picture of who God is and what He is doing and why He is doing it, the better they can learn to make application to the unique aspects of their lives. In other words, big-picture truth can go very deep and allows for specific application in a diverse group, but small-picture truth must be wide and shallow. More about that later.

 Missional student ministry leads students to fulfill the mission of God through the gospel of God regardless of vocation or location.

A second distinctive given by the Missional Church Network is that **the missional church is about the church being incarnational rather than attractional**. This means being the presence of Christ, living out the gospel in how we relate to others at public schools, in our neighborhoods, jobs, and relationships. Yes, invite people to weekly church services and seasonal events (attractional). But also invite them into your daily lives to experience a relationship with God (incarnational). Jesus was sent into the world as God in the flesh. Our resurrected Lord then sent the church as His body to make disciples of every nation. Every believer has the Spirit of Christ empowering him or her for this great mission, and that includes teenagers. Missional student ministry will focus on being incarnational much more than on hosting attractional events.

Student ministry has too often been run on the engine of events, so that in practice a given ministry moves like a roller coaster, up the hill with the next event, flying down the tracks in a blur as the event happens, and then the arduous trek back up the next hill only to fly down once again. Events do matter and can be used to help create a missional view. But the obsession with them, and the utilization of events as the key scorecard for success, must not drive our ministry.

Biblically, the call from God is to make disciples as we go, not gather a crowd in one place. Look at the book of Acts. There were definitely large crowds at times where the gospel was preached. But these crowds came because of the work of God, not because of a great job of advertising. And the crowds often thinned as Jesus spoke of the cost of discipleship. As we seek to make disciples, we will recognize increasingly how stunts to appease a crowd matter far less than believers living incarnationally, investing in their world as Christ came to live among us, in their communities.

The final distinctive outlined by the Missional Church Network is that **the missional church focuses on the mission of God, or the *missio Dei*.** In other words, those with a missional perspective no longer see the church "service" as the primary connecting point for those outside the church. While we want the lost to become Christ followers in the context of a local faith family, the church, our primary goal is not to get students into a building but to get them to Christ. The missional church is a "sent people" more concerned with sending the people of the church out among the people of the world than with getting the people of the world in among the people of the church. As Emil Brunner famously stated, "The church exists by mission, just as fire exists by burning."[5] For example, missional student ministry cares more about making an impact on the local public school than filling up a room at the church. Others have described this distinction as a challenge to "go and be" as opposed to "come and see. We must reject the Christian subculture that lives as though God only works in a church building or in our Christian meetings. God is at work in His world, not just in the church (especially the church building!). Rather than having a missions committee as a part of the church, or a missions focus as part of student ministry, we see the mission of God as being the center of all we do: Every activity, trip, what and how we teach, everything from calendar to content, flows from the redemptive mission of God.

As I write this, our daughter Hannah recently graduated from a massive public school in our town. Getting the majority of those students to a big rally would be extremely difficult. And, once there, many of these students have so little gospel understanding that even the most effective of gospel communicators would not reach them in a one-time event. Some would be reached, and I am personally for any method that will help people come to Christ. But here is the other side of "successful" one-time events: They cause us to value those we have reached while not focusing on the many we have not. For instance, there were more than five hundred seniors in my daughter's class. I would guess that at least 80 percent did not know Christ. If we have a great event to which we were able to get half of them to come, and the Lord saved one hundred of them, we would consider that a marvelous thing. At the same time, we need to reach the remaining 250. The best way to reach those would be to have teachers and students leading gospel-centered lives on the campus as missionaries, which can be done daily whether these students ever attend an event or not.

Students in their middle and high school years are not merely adolescents, or children finishing their childhood years; they are young men and women moving toward impact in the adult world. Therefore, if you are a minister in the local church, you must not think of yourself as simply a Bible teacher or leader; you must think like a missionary strategist, equipping students to know the gospel and the culture and to live as missionaries.

This means we seek to create a missional posture in the students we lead. How? Here is a list from the Missional Church Network that offers a good place to start:[6]

**Spiritual formation/transformation.** How we teach believers, whether middle schoolers or senior adults, will focus on life transformation, not merely information dissemination. Spiritual formation becomes the goal more than teaching a lesson. This will mean a radical refocus on how most churches do Bible study, weekly meetings, and other activities.

**Emphasize the priesthood of believers.** In using this expression, Martin Luther meant that Christians are to live out their faith in every area of life. Whether you are a butcher, baker, or candlestick maker, a student, an athlete, or a teacher, your life and ministry are as vital as the pastor's or anyone else's. This includes students, not just older adults.

This applies particularly to current student ministry, because most youth are treated more like grade-school children than young men and women. Helping them see the value of living for Christ no matter what their career may be is vital to a growing missional reformation in the Western church.

**Change the scorecard.** Student ministry too often measures by numbers and events exclusively. Numbers matter. The Scriptures record a lot of numbers. But we are in danger of becoming like David, who sinned when he numbered the people, if we rate our success by numbers in the building rather than the lost around us.

Our scorecard should measure the impact we are making in the local public school as much as (or more than!) the numbers we have in our youth gathering. How many students are sharing their faith? How many are volunteering at the school? How are students in your ministry cultivating relationships with unchurched youth? How are their families doing? How are they living for Christ after leaving the student ministry?

This won't happen without longevity in leadership. With the average tenure of one and a half years for a student pastor, change will rarely occur.

**Value "third places."** Jesus Christ did not come to establish a moral code; He came to launch a movement. I am sitting in a Starbucks in Saint Augustine, Florida, as I type this. Today young people by the thousands stand in long lines, pay highly inflated prices, and go out of their way to meet friends at Starbucks. Why? Because Starbucks created what sociologists call a *third place* (home, school, third place). Starbucks grew globally in a short period of time because it quickly had the feel of a movement, and people who go there do not feel the same about going to McDonald's or Burger King as they do going to Starbucks, although McDonald's has adapted to create coffee products and more of a café feel because of places like Starbucks.

Starbucks sees itself less as a coffee company serving people and more as a people company serving coffee. Millennials get the difference.

Starbucks has become the epitome of a third place for students. Everywhere I go I see students passionate about meeting friends there. They do not go to Starbucks because of the products they sell, but because of the environment they create. I constantly encourage pastors and student pastors to spend less time in the church office and more time in the third places in their community. At a time when it is becoming more difficult for student pastors to meet with students at public schools, God has given us third places instead. I have had plenty of meetings with young adults, neighbors, and others in third places to talk about the gospel.

Our culture has become post-Christian. More and more unbelievers must be engaged with the gospel away from a church building. If we are serious about reaching youth, this is critical. This includes understanding the place of hospitality and the need to love and welcome unchurched students who may not "get" everything we do.

**Give students the metanarrative.** The overarching Story of

Scripture — the metanarrative of Creation, Fall, Rescue, Restoration — helps students see how all of reality relates to the work of God in our world, not just our "spiritual" lives. Show students that although Jesus certainly came to give us the hope of heaven after death, He came to give us life now as well. I believe this to be so crucial that it is the main point of chapter 2 and the foundation of much of the book.

## THE REALITY: THE BAR IS TOO LOW

A few years ago, I found myself hitting the big 5-0 in age, overweight, tired, and a legend at making excuses. I had an artificial hip, after all, so how could I exercise? I travel a lot, eat out, and have a pretty sedentary lifestyle. I was doomed to be yet another fat preacher, I thought. But my recognition of the status quo in my life, becoming honest with my excuses and my present reality, led me to a pursuit of change. Now, three years later and almost forty pounds lighter, thanks to P90X and the encouragement of many students, I am in better shape today than I was a decade ago.

We must take an honest inventory of student ministry, not to whine but to be intentional and effective in the change we seek. We minister today to the largest number of young people in the history of the United States. And we are part of a remarkable youth expansion globally as well. But the status quo attitude toward youth must change. As I wrote in *Raising the Bar*,[7] we must stop perceiving teens as immature and begin to see them as young adults with great potential for the kingdom.

Our perspective on students needs to change. I will focus mainly on positive change in our time, but we must be honest about where we are. The general posture the church, including parents and student ministry in general, has taken toward students comes more from MTV and ABC Family than either Scripture or history.

David Balkan argues that adolescence — or as my colleague David Alan Black calls it, the "myth of adolescence" — arose during the

Industrial Revolution as (1) compulsory education laws put education in the hands of the state, not parents; (2) child labor laws made it illegal to work in factories before a certain age; and (3) the juvenile justice system separated younger from older criminals.[8] Kenda Creasy Dean adds that the notion of an in-between time from childhood to adulthood came in the twentieth century, an "invention of the Industrial Revolution" to keep younger workers from displacing older.[9] Further, adolescence arose as public education created an "age-stratification of American society (which allowed advertisers to target youth as a 'market')," which then allowed for the milieu where "the American 'teenager' — a post-World War II youth with free time and disposable income — was born."[10]

Novels such as *The Catcher in the Rye* and *Lord of the Flies* in the early 1950s, along with movies like *Rebel Without a Cause,* recognized and at times glorified rebellious youth. On the heels of this gradual shift in culture came the rise of rock music with its posture of protest, a genre allowing students to behave not like young adults but like . . . well, like adolescents. Eventually this shift led to the culture of adolescence we now see. And much of student ministry adopts this posture rather than speaking truth into it.

I am by no means arguing that a fifteen-year-old can make the same decisions and application of Scripture to life as a fifty-year-old, or a twenty-five-year-old, for that matter. But as I noted in *Raising the Bar*, we could almost universally in our churches expect more out of students than we do currently.

The practical impact of adolescent theory in the culture and in the church is twofold: It encourages teens to act like grade-school children instead of young adults; and it encourages the notion that the teen years of necessity are a time of rebellion, narcissism, and evildoing, aka "sowing wild oats."

This creates a self-fulfilling prophecy patterned more after MTV than the Bible, and we often get exactly what we expect. No wonder we have so many young adults in their twenties and thirties today who have a difficult time functioning as adults. We have told them they do not have to be mature, and far too often they have become what we expected. We can expect students to grasp the gospel, to make responsible decisions, and to make an impact for the glory of God while in their teens. But there is another problem we must address before we move forward, as it affects the very way we teach the Bible to students.

## MORALISTIC THERAPEUTIC DEISM

Student ministers know this term well, or at least they should. Christian Smith and Melinda Denton have popularized this term out of a massive research project called the National Study of Youth and Religion.[11] Smith and Denton detail the idea of Moralistic Therapeutic Deism extensively in a book called *Soul Searching*, published from their findings.[12]

Smith and Denton argue that the Western church has done a phenomenal job of communicating to students. But what has been communicated has not been as biblically centered as we might hope. We have communicated Christianity as behavior modification too often and as the matchless work of a grace-bearing God who is the center of it all too little. In her presentation of the findings of the study, Kenda Creasy Dean observed, "The National Study of Youth and Religion reveals a theological fault line running underneath American churches: an adherence to a do-good, feel-good spirituality that has little to do with the Triune God of Christian tradition and even less to do with loving Jesus Christ enough to follow him into the world."[13]

In other words, Dean argues that this study shows the very way many of us have raised children in our churches has worked against any sort of missional impulse we might hope to engage. This is no small charge. She adds, "American young people are unwittingly being formed into an imposter faith that poses as Christianity, but that in fact lacks the holy desire and missional clarity necessary for Christian discipleship."[14]

What has been taught, this thing they call Moralistic Therapeutic Deism, has offered a how-to faith based on the needs of the individual over the redemptive plan of the Creator God. How has this happened, often in churches that stand on the Bible as the Word of God? I would argue part of this comes from our tendency to view students as "kids" who are more silly than serious, as already mentioned. In addition, we have fundamentally shifted much of our teaching and living of Scripture from seeing the Bible through the lens of the gospel and the mission of God to understanding the Bible primarily as a road map that will guide us via morality to the place of faithfully serving God.

Unfortunately, many churches have taught the Bible to children and youth not as a book with one central, redemptive message (see chapter 2), but as a collection of stories and morals with the gospel as the key story. Moralistic Therapeutic Deism is "moralistic" because its focus is behavior modification. In a subtle way, acting right becomes more important than believing right. It is "therapeutic," for it focuses on surface change, turning the Bible into a counseling manual more than the revelation of God. It is "deistic" because it does not require a God who is intimately involved in all of Creation and in all aspects of our lives, but a God who generally exists to bring us happiness, most specifically in our spiritual lives.

I call it the Aesop's Fables approach to the Bible. It is ironically a "moral failure," for by focusing on morality too much we actually hinder students from seeing the lifelong, holistic implications of their faith. Motivation for serving God stems more from changing our behavior than from living a life of radical faith. Such extrinsic motivation will actually work in the short term: Show students how sex before marriage will lead to guilt and disease, for instance, or show them how lying will cost them friendships, and they will abstain from these sins, at least for a season. But if moral change becomes the primary focus of our faith, the long-term obedience we seek may actually be the one thing we will not see.

It could well be that our short-term focus is contributing to students' dropping out of church. But the much-debated topic of dropout rates actually fails to emphasize a more critical point, because even those who remain in our churches lack the missional drive to make gospel impact in their daily lives. In other words, how many who stay "in church" still "drop out" of active, daily, missional faith?

All this is not to say that behavioral change is unimportant. Our morality marks a vital part of being conformed to the image of Christ. But a growing sense of moral uprightness and concomitant behavior reflecting this is a result of our faith; it simply cannot be the prime motivator. We have confused the point (the indicative) with the result (the imperative), and this has not helped us in discipling students. The way we teach the Bible may in fact hinder our missional focus.

For instance, instead of seeing the story of David as all Scripture does, tied closely to the story of redemption and the coming of the Messiah, we take a story like David and Goliath and moralize it, and in so doing we actually marginalize it. We preach about how David killed Goliath, so we can now defeat those pesky enemies in our lives. Or, Joseph's brothers victimized him and yet God used him, so Joseph's story becomes a means of therapy for those who have been hurt. Yet when we read the story of Joseph from the perspective of all of Scripture and the message of redemption throughout, we see his vital role in the mission of God to save sinners. That is not to say we cannot learn practical advice from David's defeat of a giant or Joseph's determined faith to resist sexual temptation; but it is to say we can miss the greater point of these narratives by turning them into individual stories with a moral. These are not parables; they help us connect with the plan of God in eternity.

The practical result of turning the Bible into a series of moral truths is to make assumptions about the gospel and minimize its role in our lives. We move the good news of Jesus' death and resurrection to the category of "lost person only," so that the gospel is for unbelievers, not believers. So we have our mega youth events and we share the gospel (or often tack it on at the end), but we do not teach the impact of the gospel for the believer and the redemptive story of God in all of the Bible, and thus its impact on all of life. So students grow up in church, learn a lot of stories, and live their lives with Jesus at the periphery. They never get the border of the puzzle of life by understanding the mission of God; they simply get practical stories on how to deal with certain felt needs, and they get their eternal destiny taken care of, or so they think. Many become the dechurched—those who grow up in the church but walk away when separated from the familiar (family, home church, and so on). Others spiritually limp their way through life, never getting the great plan of God for creation and for their lives.

A focus on Christianity as Moralistic Therapeutic Deism explains why so many believers today confuse biblical Christianity with civil religion and the spiritual war for winning the souls of men with the cultural wars of winning political arguments. We read of how young people played critical roles in earlier seasons of revival, and those movements had a searing-hot devotion to the gospel of Jesus Christ. If we are to have a missional movement in our time, it may manifest itself in many ways practically, but it will be birthed out of gospel fervor, not moral failure.

▶ The Bible is not mainly a book about morality; it is a book about reality.

While we recognize issues that have brought us to the place of treating students like children and teaching the Bible like a morality play, let us shift our thinking to see the great opportunity before us.

Suzanne Collins captivated much of the sentiment of this generation with her remarkable storytelling in *The Hunger Games* trilogy. In book 1, we read of how the drunken Haymitch must help lead the young heroes Katniss and Peeta not only to survival but to victory, as the two destinations could not be separated. Despite his penchant for a perpetual state of inebriation, Haymitch ultimately did provide key counsel and aid in the mission his two protégés shared.

Unlike *The Hunger Games*, we do not live in a fictitious world in the future. We live in a real world now. But we have an even greater task, and that is to provide training and support for a generation of young people who have a much greater mission than survival. Yet it seems we often focus on helping students survive in a broken world instead of succeeding in their mission. Like Haymitch, we must not only help students survive, we must help them fulfill the mission, and in so doing, find life.

And thus we begin a journey to see the world as missionaries and, as we go, to equip the students we know to do the same.

## REVIEW AND APPLICATION

- What is missional? Do your students understand the term?
- What does a missional student ministry look like? What are its features?
- Can you see examples of the Bible being taught today as a book of moral stories instead of being about God's mission?
- In Matthew 4:19 Jesus said, "Follow me, and I will make you fishers of men." Can you see a missional idea in this verse? How?

# CHAPTER 2

# MISSIONAL IDEA

## *Berlin, Germany*

I have never been to Berlin, but I have been to Germany, the nation that has shaped Western civilization in the modern era. If you could journey to Germany today, you would see a place that is very different from the tumultuous nation of the twentieth century. Germany epitomizes in our time the positive impact of change. Go back a few decades and witness the horror of Jews exterminated under the evil of Nazism. I recall the Iron Curtain and the Cold War, symbolized by the wall between a divided Berlin. But one day the wall came down, and when it did, everything changed.

In his book *Gospel Wakefulness*, Jared Wilson compares the revolutionary change that happens when we truly grasp the wonder of the gospel with the dramatic sociopolitical change that came with the fall of the Berlin Wall:

> In the well-appointed study of a professor of history in a prestigious university in the American South sits a brick-sized piece of the Berlin Wall. It sits on the floor, because he uses it as a doorstop. He is not ignorant of the piece's historical significance; as a historian he is deeply informed of the struggle and the repression attached to the

wall, to the shame it symbolized and the division both literal and cultural it created. He not only knows about but also teaches on the international reverberations that occurred when the great emblem of the communist stronghold in Western Europe finally came down. . . .

In a small, dingy apartment in Midwest America lives an elderly immigrant woman who sells newspapers and fresh cut flowers during the day and cleans an office building in the evenings. On an iron shelf in her bedroom sits a small lidless glass jar, and in that jar is a piece of the Berlin Wall the size of a marble. She has often held that piece of rock in her withered hand and wept. Her husband did not live to see the wall come down. Her cousin was one of the estimated five thousand people who tried to escape from the communist Eastern Bloc into West Berlin. He was one of the estimated one hundred to two hundred people killed by border guards in the attempt. He was one of those crushed by the Iron Curtain, so she is one of those who knows the unique confluence of memorial pain and joy in having intimately felt how the world once was and in having experienced how the whole world was changed. She knows what it feels like to carry an ocean full of grief and longing, what it feels like to cling to a sliver of hope, and what it feels like when that sliver of hope — a crack in the great barrier of darkness — gives way to a dam break of glorious fulfillment and release.

When the professor hears the epic Brandenburg Gate speech in which President Ronald Reagan famously commanded, "Mr. Gorbachev, tear down this wall!" he admires it as a watershed moment in history, as iconic a sound bite from the annals of history as any. When the woman hears "Mr. Gorbachev, tear down this wall!" she is stirred, always. When the professor speaks of the fall of the Berlin Wall as an earth-shattering event, he really does mean to communicate the radical nature of the event; he really does understand this. But the woman knows that the fall of the Berlin Wall was an earth-shattering event *deep down in her bones*."[1]

This, Wilson writes, is gospel wakefulness.

Not enough students know and experience this wakefulness, this wonder of the gospel today in our churches and student ministries.

We need a revolution, a tearing down of a functional Berlin Wall in the church. And I believe it is coming. In some places, it already has. But even as the fall of the Berlin Wall started not with a sledge-hammer but an idea, the shift that must come in student ministry will not come from another great event or program, but from a recovery of the gospel.

We put up walls by compartmentalizing the gospel, picking and choosing the parts we like or understand. But Christianity cannot be reduced to any one aspect of its reality:

- The gospel changes behavior, but reducing its effect to behavior modification hides its truth in legalism. The gospel doesn't create Pharisees; we do.
- The gospel sets one free, but emphasizing freedom apart from surrender to Christ and His commands traps those freed by it to antinomianism. The gospel sets you free to follow Christ.
- The gospel is truth, and propositional truth for that matter, but reducing it to a series of propositions hides the amazing wonder of the new birth and a relationship with the Most High God.
- The gospel shows us how to do the very thing we are created to do: worship. But teaching worship as something done mostly in a service guided by particular forms loses the wonder of worship in our preferences and creates division, not unity.

The gospel of Jesus Christ is much bigger than any of its individual nuances. Before we can send forth missionaries, we must first be sure they know what their mission is, a mission built on conviction about an unchanging gospel. Before we get to the *imperative*, we need to understand the *indicative*. In other words, before we can apply the message of Christianity to our daily lives, we must be sure we understand what that message is and not assume the students in our churches (or their families) get it.

> If you want to build a ship, don't summon people to buy wood, prepare tools, distribute jobs, and organize the work; rather teach people the yearning for the wide, boundless ocean. — Antoine de Saint-Exupéry[2]

Student ministry, like any ministry of a church, Christian family, or individual believer, must be centered on a robust grasp of the heart of our faith: the gospel. As my friend J. D. Greear so eloquently says in his book *Gospel*, "Being able to articulate the gospel with accuracy is one thing; having its truth captivate your soul is quite another."[3] In my view it makes the difference between students who just survive the teen years versus students who live missionally for all of life. And it should be the bar to which all student ministries aspire. However, we too often get sidetracked on one aspect of our faith that threatens the heart of that faith.

## IDEAS CHANGE THE WORLD

As a freshman in college, my son, Josh, told me how he had suddenly learned to enjoy reading. When I asked what had caused a shift of interest, he showed me a book he was assigned before the next semester. I looked at some of the things he wrote in the margins, and then looked at the cover. It was Plato's *Republic*, one of the key works in the history of ideas. Why did Plato intrigue him? I told him that a hundred years from now no one will remember Oprah Winfrey or Rush Limbaugh. But in great schools they will still require students to read Plato. Why? Ideas have power. Ideas change the world.

Great awakenings in the past centered on the idea that the gospel was worthy of proclamation and incarnation. Young people played prominent roles in these movements. John Wesley, George Whitefield, and others confronted ritualistic religion in the Anglican Church, while Jonathan Edwards confronted a similarly lifeless faith. Today we have so oversimplified Christianity, assuming people have some general awareness of biblical truth, that we need to recover the greatness of the gospel.

While not always embraced, there was a time when the great Story of the creating and redeeming God was certainly understood by most in our land. Not any longer. Gabe Lyons states, "The Christian narrative has been almost completely replaced by a new story,"[4] while Kenda Dean refers to an "imposter faith that poses as Christianity, but that in fact lacks the holy desire and missional clarity for Christian discipleship."[5] At best, the Christian narrative has simply become one of many, no more significant in the public square than other world religions, atheistic philosophies, political ideologies, or even pop-culture values.

## WHAT IDEA DRIVES YOUR STUDENT MINISTRY?

Is it pragmatism that says numbers matter above all, to the point that you will sacrifice truth to get people to a building? Is it making young people like you? Likely not. But is it the gospel, and is that clear to all? Does the idea behind your ministry explain all reality, or is it simply a means to describe your religious activity?

Missional means showing unbelievers the gospel from the perspective of their worldview, moving them to see a biblical idea. This is what Paul did at Mars Hill in Acts 17, as we'll further explore in later chapters. Because the Bible is true, and the gospel explains the great questions of life (How did it all begin? What went wrong? What can be done? What does the future hold?), the central idea of Scripture applies to all areas of life. For example, students love movies. Hollywood can hardly be described as evangelical in its posture, yet filmmakers create movie after movie that give us an opportunity to point people to the gospel. Think about some common plotlines of movies and stories. A man falls in a hole and is rescued. Sounds uninspiring, but people make millions on movies with that story line, in particular action stories like *Braveheart* or *The Lord of the Rings*. Or try this one: Boy meets girl, things are exciting, then things go badly, but in the end boy gets girl and they both find happiness. Pretty much every romantic comedy (think Tom Hanks and Matthew McConaughey, for instance) follows that story line. Or here is one we all love: rags to riches. You know, *Cinderella*, *The Princess Diaries*, and others in which someone in an unfortunate situation finds their way out.

From *The Lord of the Rings* to the Harry Potter series to *The Hunger Games*, story after story points us to a general plot: Things typically start off pretty well, then things go badly, often involving a villain, followed by a resolution, often involving a rescuer or hero, and the proverbial ending, "and they all lived happily ever after."

The story line I gave you above follows the basic story line of Scripture. And why do we have such a hunger for a happy ending? Because we seek that which only the gospel can give. How can it be that great stories in literature or film that seemingly have nothing to do with Christianity actually illustrate its core idea? Because the Bible is not primarily a book about *morality*, but about *reality*.

Students should be shown how the gospel—the heart and soul of Christianity—defines reality, the reality that matters most. In fact, all reality fails to make sense unless we see it through the lens of Christ and His work. Experiencing this Gospel Story should not only drive our ministries but our lives.

## THE GRAND IDEA OF SCRIPTURE

In Luke 24, the risen Lord explained the central idea of Scripture in His conversation with the disciples on the road to Emmaus in verses 44-48. In this passage He told them that everything in Moses, the Psalms, and the Prophets, meaning all the Scripture they had, must be fulfilled. And then He told them what these Scriptures say: that the Christ must suffer and rise from the dead, and that repentance and the forgiveness of sins will be preached to the nations. Jesus makes crystal clear the redeeming mission of God through all of Scripture. Similarly, in 1 Corinthians 15, Paul related Christ's death, burial, and resurrection to all the Scriptures.

The mission of God is central to all of Scripture, all of creation, all of history, and therefore, all of life. Jesus and His work on the cross speaks to everything from attitude (see Philippians 2) to forgiveness (see Ephesians 4), from how we understand finances (see 2 Corinthians 8) to how we deal with sexual temptation (see 1 Corinthians 6), or from how we deal with disciple making (see 2 Timothy 2:1-2) to how we understand marriage (see Ephesians 5:25). Our encouragement in facing persecution for Christ is the gospel (see Acts 4:23-31), and our instruction in how to live all of life (see 2 Corinthians 10:9-21) is found in the gospel. Give students the message of God so they can spend their lives living out the mission of God.

A few years ago, I took a different approach to looking at Scripture and sharing the good news with others. I shifted from trying to share as brief a summary as I could with people to telling them the great, epic Story of the gospel seen in Scripture. I realized most people I talked with had no clear idea of what the Bible's message is, but saw it as a reference book for problems or a guide for morality. Where does the gospel start? With a virgin birth? At the cross? According to Luke 24:44-48, Jesus said all Scripture from Moses forward points to His work on the cross. Unlike Moralistic Therapeutic Deism, which separates the Bible into individual stories for moral training, for Jesus there is one message in Scripture, all of Scripture, and that message is the gospel.

▶ The redemptive plotline in Scripture: Creation, Fall, Rescue, Restoration.

When viewing the gospel from the perspective of all of Scripture, we see four parts to the plotline: Creation, Fall, Rescue, and Restoration. We have tended to share somewhat about the Fall and focused specifically on the rescue, or redemption. And indeed this is part of the heart and soul of the Gospel Story. But in a post-Christian world, we must see the gospel in its fullness. Lyons understands this: "The truncated Gospel that is often recounted is faithful to the fall and redemption pieces of the story, but largely ignores the creation and restoration components. These missing elements are at the heart of what a new generation of Christians are relearning, and subsequently, retelling."[6]

## CREATION

The Bible begins in Genesis. The Bible's message, the revelation from God to man, starts in the beginning with God, who creates. Read the gospel of John. You know, the one we print up separately and give to our unbelieving friends? Where does it start? With God, and creation. Look at Romans. Remember the "Roman Road" to salvation? I have used it. We start with Romans 3:23. But hold on. In Romans 1:20 as Paul is only beginning his amazing description of salvation through Christ's gospel, he says that in creation, God's "invisible attributes" are available for all to see.

Creation.

I fear what we do too often in speaking of the gospel with unbelievers is ask them to step into the Gospel Story in the middle of it, without the context that we assume: that God is great, glorious, and the Creator of all. Walk into the showing of a movie halfway through the picture, watch ten minutes, then leave. Will you understand the whole story? Not likely. We live in Athens today, not Jerusalem, and we like Paul at Mars Hill must back up and give a larger perspective to the gospel. This is a helpful way to show students who know Christ how the gospel is related to all reality and not just their separated church lives. It also shows unbelievers how the gospel relates to the reality they see every day.

Think about nature around us. Our world is amazing. I just returned from the Florida Keys, where my wife, Michelle, and I observed some of the most beautiful scenery in the world. And life—there is such a harmony to all of created life. When I ask my students each semester to name the place they think of when they want to get away and spend uninterrupted time with God, 99 percent name a pristine pocket of creation: the mountains, a forest, or the beach. There is something wondrous about stepping into a scene that portrays the wonder of creation. I have seen the Sistine Chapel and Notre Dame Cathedral, and walked through the Louvre in Paris. None compares to sitting on the shore of the Indian Ocean far, far away from civilization.

Creation.

You see, our fundamental problem is our view of God. We are too easily tempted to think of God first from our perspective. In so doing we shrink God to our level. As a result we tend to make the Bible more about us than about God. Instead, we should see God from the perspective we read in Hebrews 1:1-3:

> Long ago, at many times and in many ways, God spoke to our fathers by the prophets, but in these last days he has spoken to us by his Son, whom he appointed the heir of all things, through whom also he created the world. He is the radiance of the glory of God and the exact imprint of his nature, and he upholds the universe by the word of his power.

This God holds everything together by the sheer word of His power. This God has revealed Himself in His Son, Jesus, who has made purification for our sins. Leaders both inside the institutional church and on the fringes of orthodoxy have a tendency to shrink God and elevate us. We all do this—it is the essence of sin. This is one reason Scripture often takes us back to the majesty of creation (see Genesis 1:1; John 1:1; Romans 1:20).

Creation has been made with some remarkable order. Plants provide oxygen for us; we give them carbon dioxide. Without either, we would all perish. Students in high school learn the balance in creation and the role plants, herbivores, and carnivores play in it. Consider something as unexpected as snakes. If there were no snakes we would be covered up with rats. You may not like snakes, but no one wants a house full of rats either! I have kept many as pets, so I am partial to snakes. If you just can't bring yourself to think about snakes, consider the eagle. One eagle eats a hundred trout in a year, which eat ten thousand grasshoppers, which eat one million blades of grass. A million blades of grass to support one eagle. Amazing.[7]

The Bible says God created all this, and He made it good (see Genesis 1; John 1; Hebrews 11:3). You do not have to be a follower of Christ to see this all around us.

So God made all in creation. And He made people in His image. Don't miss this. We are much closer to God in creation than we are to the primates. He created us to worship Him and gave us an amazing world in which to do so. We are remarkably distinguished from the rest of creation. Look at the civilizations we create, the innovations we invent, the medical and technological advances we achieve. A bird may make a nest, but it will not make a high-rise apartment complex. A chimpanzee may learn to ride a skateboard, but it will never produce a blog or question the problem of evil.

But there is more. We were made to worship. We are all glory chasers, or as Paul Tripp puts it, "glory junkies," seeking something bigger than us and beyond us worthy of supreme devotion.[8] And we do worship. As Augustine said, "Thou hast made us for thyself, and our hearts are restless until they find rest in thee."[9] We crave more. We want a happy ending. We seek fulfillment. We hate cheating and injustice. There is, as Pascal said, a God-shaped hole in all of us, unlike anything else in creation. So the Story of the Bible is that God has made an amazing creation and put us in the center of it to worship and fellowship with Him. We are stewards of all creation, and we were made to walk with God.

## FALL

But something went badly wrong. This beautiful world is broken: Death looms near us; cancer, heart failure, and disease engulf us. Tsunamis kill thousands in one place, while an earthquake does the same in another. The same mind in a man that can find the cure for a disease can also plot great evil. When Adam and Eve sinned, the Fall came and all creation was broken as a result (see Genesis 3).

In the beginning everything did what it was intended to do and did it well. But when Adam sinned, humanity fell. Soon murder, idolatry, and everything imaginable that could be wrong developed from the poison of sin. This is why parents never have to teach their children to lie or steal. It is in their nature. We have to teach children honesty and integrity. All because of the Fall.

So death entered the human race because of the Fall. We are dead in sin (see Ephesians 2) because of the Fall. The impact for us is seen in that, although created in the image of God to worship God, we now have a twisted view in which we seek to worship idols of our own making instead of the Creator (see Romans 1:18-32).

Creation has been broken and yearns for redemption (see Romans 8:22), yet we have evil in our hearts. The God who made this beautiful world is now also its rightful judge.

Creation. Fall.

## RESCUE

I'm so glad the Story did not end there! We want happy endings to stories because we know something is wrong. God moved to make a beautiful world. The very ones He made to worship Him chose to sin and rebel. But what did God do? God moved—but not away from His rebellious creation as might seem natural to us in our fallen, selfish condition. He moved to create us, and He has moved to rescue us. Jesus Christ, God Himself, became man, born of the virgin Mary (see John 1:14). He lived a sinless life. He came not mainly to teach or heal individuals; He came to die for sin. He became our substitute, bearing the weight of sin on the cross (see Romans 3:21-26; 5:8; 2 Corinthians 5:21; 1 Peter 3:18). Philippians 2 describes the wonderful condescension, where God became man to pay for our sins. This is the wonderful news of the gospel!

All this relates to the mission of God in our day. There is a "relationship between the *imago Dei* (the image of God) and the *missio Dei* (the mission of God)," Francis Dubose has written. Once sin entered the world, he added, "The whole agenda of God from this point on is aimed at the resolution of this problem."[10]

The center of our faith is a bloody cross and a glorious resurrection by which we find rescue from sin through faith in Jesus. We were legally guilty before a holy God, and through Jesus we are justified by faith. We were slaves to sin but have been redeemed by Christ (see Romans 3:24). We were dead in our sin and have been made alive by the grace of God through faith in Christ (see Ephesians 2). We were orphans who have been adopted by God (see Romans 8:15). Never get over what God has done in Christ!

God moved again, for Jesus rose from the dead. He was seen by many witnesses (see 1 Corinthians 15). Those who come to God by faith based on the work of Christ can again live out the mission of God. We can have life in His name. We can follow Jesus Christ, receive forgiveness for sin, and have an eternal hope in heaven (see Luke 24:44-47). We can have a relationship with the God who made us for His glory. We can live lives that matter. We can have the happy ending we so yearn for.

Creation. Fall. Rescue.


## RESTORATION

God has moved. God is moving to save people from sin even today. But the Bible also tells us this world is not the end. He will move again to restore all things. There is a promise of hope, of a new heaven and a new earth, of living forever in the presence of God. Revelation 21:1-4 describes it like this:

> Then I saw a new heaven and a new earth, for the first heaven and the first earth had passed away, and the sea was no more. And I saw the holy city, new Jerusalem, coming down out of heaven from God, prepared as a bride adorned for her husband. And I heard a loud voice from the throne saying, "Behold, the dwelling place of God is with man. He will dwell with them, and they will be his people, and God himself will be with them as their God. He will wipe away every tear from their eyes, and death shall be no more, neither shall there be mourning, nor crying, nor pain anymore, for the former things have passed away."

God will one day make all things new. This God has been moving and will continue to do His work. Redeemed people from every tribe, tongue, and nation will be in His presence to worship Him forever.

Creation. Fall. Rescue. Restoration. This grand drama of redemption tells the Story of God's work in history. It is recorded in much greater detail in the Bible. In fact, the Story of the Bible is the mission of God to redeem sinful people to Himself for the purpose of reflecting His glory through His image perfectly shown in the death and life of Jesus Christ. This is the greatest movement we could ever know. We can bring glory to the One who alone deserves it.

We get to be a part of that movement. Amazing. Regardless of your background, status, or ethnicity, you can join this movement. And regardless of your vocation or location, you can give your life to advancing it. Believers, especially students in this next generation, love this revelation. Lyons observed that they "enjoy Scripture as they believe it was meant to be: a grand narrative that tells a story of a God who loves and pursues, rescues, gives grace, and goes to any length to restore relationships with his most prized creations."[11]

As my friend Mark Liederbach likes to put it, life is worship. We all worship. But most do not worship the One who created us to worship Him. But when we do become worshippers of God through the work of Jesus Christ on the cross, life becomes *missional* worship, or worship focused on inviting others to join the movement of worshipping our Creator. That is the movement I have given my life to spread.[12]

Have you come to know this God? Has He changed your life and set you free? If so, you now have purpose not centered on you, but on Him. You were created to worship God. When you become His follower by faith, you become part of a gospel-centered movement of redemption. You and I have the great honor of spending our lives — regardless of what job, economic setting, ethnic origin, or advantages and disadvantages we have experienced — living out and sharing the amazing good news found in Jesus Christ.

We live and work and play and raise our families in the context of that grand movement of God. You have one chance to live your life, one shot at leading in His movement. Sadly, in the Western church so many followers of Christ have lost their vision for advancing this movement, choosing comfortable church buildings over the less comfortable practice of sharing this Gospel Story with others.

People with whom I share who don't know Christ agree with me that we live in an amazing world. They also concur that something awful has happened in our world. I can get into a serious gospel conversation simply by talking about obvious things around us. Then the cross of Christ becomes more than a religious symbol for one world religion (the way many unchurched perceive it); it fits into a larger understanding of how everything works. That does not mean everyone will suddenly repent and believe, because our will is a stubborn thing. But it has proven remarkably helpful in communicating the good news in a larger context to unbelievers.

It also helps me to share with the growing numbers of dechurched: those (especially young adults) who have grown up in church, moved into the adult world, and have no use for it anymore. This helps me to show them how sometimes, though not intentionally, churches have taught the Bible as a collection of moral truisms instead of the revelation of God to men. Several times in the past few months I have spoken to dechurched young adults who have told me something like, "I never quite got this from my days in church."

We must see that our world today inside and outside the church has been too focused on itself and missed the wonder, greatness, and splendor of our God. Beginning with the majesty of creation and moving to the wonder of the cross has proven helpful to me in opening people's eyes.

 A helpful resource for understanding the whole narrative of the gospel in Scripture and to share it with others is The Story at www.viewthestory.com.

## GOSPEL-CENTERED CHRISTIANITY

A businessman embarks on a journey in the first-class cabin of a train in Spain. To his delight, he finds that he's sitting next to the famous artist Pablo Picasso. Gathering up his courage, he turns to the master and says, "Senor Picasso, you are a great artist, but why is all your art, all modern art, so screwed up? Why don't you paint reality instead of these distortions?"

Picasso hesitates for a moment and asks, "So what do you think reality looks like?"

The man grabs his wallet and pulls out a picture of his wife. "Here, like this. It's my wife."

Picasso takes the photograph, looks at it, and grins. "Really? She's very small. And flat, too."[13]

Leadership means defining reality, and reality means more than a simple two-dimensional snapshot of the world, even though the snapshot may be true. We have too often reduced the wonder and majesty of the gospel of Jesus Christ to a simple snapshot from a wallet while trying to present Him to a world that sees things more like Picasso. While a true representation as far as it goes, it so reduces the gospel that it easily misses its greatness.

When students see the greatness of the gospel and how it changes everything, they are well on their way to becoming a part of God's great missional movement.

It is true that one can understand the gospel as a few propositions from Romans à la the Roman Road. But to take an unbeliever who does not know Scripture, understand who God is, or comprehend the depths of depravity, then offer him quick bullet points as the whole gospel is no different from offering a two-dimensional picture of my wife as a fair representation of who she is. Visually, it represents her to some extent. But you know nothing of her personality, her wisdom, or her story if you only see a snapshot.

I have led people to Christ using the Roman Road. Without exception they have been people with a background in the Scriptures, with some awareness of the greatness of the gospel beyond its propositions. And the traditional Roman Road presentation begins with Romans 3:23, assuming people get the earlier part. We can no longer assume that. Romans 1:20 speaks of creation, and Romans 1:18–3:20 speaks of the fall. We cannot simply extract Romans 3:23 as if Romans 1:18–3:20 did not exist. Too many unchurched people fail to understand the good news because they haven't experienced it—instead they've been offered an incomplete picture with scattered bullet points and nobody to help connect the dots.

This is why my colleague George Robinson and I have been involved in an approach called The Story to help believers understand the greatness and wonder of the gospel not only for unbelievers, but for themselves. I believe we must give people more than a snapshot of the good news; we must help them see the wonder, the artistry, the majesty of its reality.

The challenge confronting student ministry is a challenge of theology, not ability. We have not failed to communicate, but we have communicated too often and too well a superficial faith that contradicts the heart of the gospel, which calls us not to a minimal standard but to the surrender of all of life. "We are doing an exceedingly good job of teaching youth what we really believe," Kenda Creasy Dean has astutely observed. "Namely, that Christianity is not a big deal, that God requires little, and the church is a helpful social institution filled with nice people focused primarily on 'folks like us'—which, of course, begs the question of whether we are really the church at all."[14] She goes on to note how most students in our churches today cannot articulate clearly the fundamentals of our faith. While we obsess with lengthy series on dating or other topics, have we failed to give them a foundation in the glorious Gospel Story?

The opposite of Moralistic Therapeutic Deism is gospel-centered theism. We must help students see that they are not the center of the universe; we have to help them get a grasp of the sovereign God who does not exist to please them and otherwise leave them alone.

The Jesus of Scripture is not a homeboy, as a popular T-shirt purported. Nor is He a BFF. He is God, and the liberation students seek actually comes not from cozying up to an overly humanized Jesus but by surrendering to the glorified Son of God.

Here is the fundamental challenge as we disciple students. The gospel, this most amazing idea and truth in history, is not only for unsaved people to begin a life with Christ. No, salvation opens the door to go deeper. I once thought of Christianity as a climb up to the mountain of sanctification, where as we go we get better at cussing less and lusting less and better still at witnessing more and giving more and so on. But now I see that the way to growth comes from plunging into the ocean of gospel truth found throughout the pages of the Bible. The more we grasp the power of this creating God, see the evil of our own depravity, and grasp the wonder of His grace, resulting in a greater understanding of His glory, the more we will help equip students to live well.

This lies at the heart of what student ministry and, for that matter, any ministry should be about. Let me remind you by way of the story of José. The Hispanic population, particularly of Millennials, is exploding today. José represents the hope of the gospel in a young man who came from an extremely troubled home, for whom only the gospel could offer lasting hope. This is the story of a gangbanger, a PK (pastor's kid), and the gospel.

> My dad has been absent for most of my life. Like many young men, I looked for that father figure and found it in a former gang member with the Latin Kings. I was taught things and did things that now embarrass me. At one point as a teen I was framed for attempted murder as some of the gang members tried to kill one of my friends and blamed me. This caused me to cry out for God, wanting to know Him and to be set free from the gang lifestyle.
>
> At that point, I came under the influence of a godly example at my high school, a PK named Abraham. God used Abraham to lead me to Christ, a complete life change! Today, I serve God using the talent He gave me (hip-hop) to influence my peers at school.

I met José at a student pastor lunch I spoke at in Florida. His student pastor, who continues to mentor him, said this about José:

> As much as his peers love his music they're even more drawn to José, this guy who has made it his mission to make Jesus famous in his school. He and his peers have helped start one of the more impressive FCA [Fellowship of Christian Athletes] groups in our area. They meet daily before school to pray for their school. They are organizing a concert in our church to benefit a local pediatric cancer unit. All student-led. This Christmas, José chose to spend the day on the streets with the homeless population in Lakeland, where he's befriended one particular gentleman named Lucky. I'm humbled just to see what they're doing.

In the history of man, believers have often lost their way. During the period of Judges in the Old Testament, God's people continually got sidetracked by all sorts of issues of idolatry and sin. In the modern era, God's people have at various times lost their way by virtue of theological shallowness on the one hand or liberalism on the other, or through focusing more on institutions of the faith over the God who gave them to us. But there is yet hope: We also read of great spiritual awakenings that revived the church and brought her back to the gospel and to the heart of our faith.

I believe we are at one of those times in history. A lot of student ministries, parents, churches, and parachurch ministries aimed at students have lost their way. But the Josés of the world compel us to offer more than moralism; they need and want the life-changing power of the gospel. I believe students in our churches can have a vital role in the return to a robust, sacrificial, Jesus-centered faith.

## REVIEW AND APPLICATION

- What are the great ideas that guide your life?
- Do you see the great narrative of Scripture as you read the Bible? Can you think of examples of this plotline — Creation, Fall, Rescue, Restoration — in other stories you know?
- What difference does it make whether we live lives focused on the gospel or not?
- In 2 Corinthians 5:17-21 Paul talks about being a new creation in Christ with a mission of reconciliation. He ends the passage by stating the gospel again (see verse 21). How does this passage help you see how to live a gospel-centered, missional life?

# CHAPTER 3

# MISSIONAL MOVEMENT

## *Costa Mesa, California*

Chuck arose a little earlier than normal on an already warm summer day. Stepping into the morning sun, he gazed at the Pacific Ocean just to his west, overwhelmed by its vastness. A chill went down the young man's spine as he felt the weight of his yearning, a desire to see many know Christ and follow Him, but tempered by the sheer magnitude of his own insignificance.

He had come to this Southern California community to lead a small church. It seemed the right place. He had confidence in the Lord and in the Scriptures, but still he hesitated. The little band of twenty-five believers seemed awfully small on this morning. So he stared at the wonder of the ocean. And he gained confidence in God.

The year was 1965. The man's name? Chuck Smith. The church he would plant, Calvary Chapel, became a movement. Part of a larger movement of God called the Jesus Movement, this was a movement propelled by a desire to make Jesus famous. Soon Smith would initiate unique ministries, from the House of Miracles coffeehouse—a missional outpost, if you will—which reached thousands of hippies of the time, to Maranatha! Music, an early example of a fundamental shift in musical worship taken for granted in churches now. Calvary Chapel would be featured in major newsmagazines of the time. Smith eventually baptized thousands of new believers in that same Pacific Ocean.[1]

Today you will find over 1,500 Calvary Chapels across the globe, including many of the largest churches in the United States. The original Calvary Chapel currently ranks as the thirty-ninth-largest church in America.

Around 1970 a similar movement on a much smaller scale happened near Birmingham, Alabama. It too saw unchurched young adults come to Jesus. Unique ministries like a One Way Christian Night Club emerged—a converted skating rink where youth could come and find love. I met Jesus at that church. I have never forgotten when I was just a boy of eleven watching and hearing young people changed by the gospel's power. Decades later as I worked on my dissertation for a PhD, I discovered that my little church was at the time the fastest-growing small church in the Southern Baptist Convention east of the Mississippi.

But most of the students in our churches today have no idea what a movement of God looks like because they have never seen anything like that. Ironically, the same Jesus Movement that led to a revolution in music in the church and to multitudes encountering Christ also planted seeds that would lead to our need today for a fresh wind of God to move in ministries to students. The large numbers of youth coming to Christ in the early 1970s and the teeming numbers of youth in the Baby Boomer generation accelerated the growth of youth ministries that have become such a common part of church life that many today assume churches have always had a youth group and youth pastors.

Nope. Recent phenomenon. But it came about because of a movement. And now it has become institutionalized and needs a fresh wind.

## MOVEMENTS CHANGE THE WORLD

Our world has been shaped more by movements than anything else—good movements like the Civil Rights movement, the abolition of slavery, and the great awakenings, as well as bad movements like the rise of the Third Reich and recent global terrorism. Movements begin with an idea, often one that challenges the status quo, and a few who possess a relentless belief in the idea and its spread. And young adults have often been key to movements.

On an August day in 1806 a group of college students gathered under a big haystack during a thunderstorm. One of the men, Samuel Mills, proposed a mission to Asia, uttering a now-famous charge: "We can do it if we will." These college leaders formed the first international missions organizations in the United States, the American Board of Commissioners for Foreign Missions.[2] The Great Commission has been advanced globally as movements born from people like these young men have catapulted believers into action. Today a growing missional movement offers us the opportunity to challenge students to join God's gospel advance.

If you happen to be in a church or community where you fail to see the movement of God, let me remind you of how He has moved over the past century:

In the year 1900, Europe and North America comprised 82 percent of the world's Christian population. In 2005, Europe and North America comprised 39 percent of the world's Christian population with African, Asian and Latin American Christians making up 60 percent of the world's Christian population. By 2050, African, Asian and Latin American Christians will constitute 71 percent of the world's Christian population.[3]

God is moving. We who know Him must join His movement, not ask Him to join ours. A growing generation of young people today offers the potential for a great movement of God. Students now know so much more about culture and the world around them because of the Internet and media exposure. They will not follow Jesus with a passion simply because they are "supposed to." They do not adore our institutions. But they can still be awed when they meet a mighty God who has revealed to us a brilliant Savior whose care for their souls is unlike anything or anyone else they could know. They want a cause, a cause bigger than life itself. And in Christ we have just that. No movement has changed the world like the one that began with a little band of believers on the eastern side of the Roman Empire in the first century AD.

 The world has been changed more decisively by movements started by a few than by dictators ruling over many.

About two millennia ago, a man walked on this earth and started a movement that has changed the world. In fact, Jesus Christ's incarnation did not start the movement, for this movement began in the heart of God before creation (see John 1; Colossians 1). But the coming of God in flesh in the Incarnation signaled the movement of God in a way that has changed your life and mine.

After the brutal crucifixion of our Lord and His glorious resurrection, a small group of believers gathered in a big upper room in Jerusalem. How could a small band of believers on the eastern edge of the mighty Roman Empire matter? After all, this group had no political or economic power. They were a collection of marginalized individuals on the fringe of their culture. That's okay; movements that change the world normally begin at the margins, not in the center of institutions. That den of disciples, that gaggle of Galileans, that collection of Christians changed the world.

They continued a movement through the church that has now touched the world. When the gospel has been front and center in a church or tradition, the movement of God is obvious. Unfortunately, for many students today, they perceive the church not as a movement of God but as an institution of organized religion.

The time has come for a missional movement. And it is coming. In fact, for many it is already here. Writers from Alan Hirsch to Ed Stetzer, from Kenda Dean to Gabe Lyons, from Mark Driscoll to Reggie McNeal, and a host of others, write today about the changing focus of the church from maintenance to missional. Students today, weary of watered-down Bible studies and being treated like grade-school kids, want more. They want truth; they want their lives to matter. They want to be part of something bigger than themselves.

Something as big as the mission of God.

▶ At its heart, Christianity is not an institution to be maintained; it is a movement to be advanced.

While many today think of Christianity in its organized and institutional sense, in its essence Christianity is still today what it was at its inception—a movement:

- A movement focusing on God's work in the world, in particular through the person of Jesus Christ, God's Son.
- A movement reflective of God's work to create all we see and know, and its movement toward God's greater purposes.
- A movement for which countless followers of Christ have suffered and many, even today, have died.
- A movement centered not on a Western lifestyle or on what we can get from God, but on salvation offered in Jesus Christ through His work on the cross, dying as a substitute for our own sin, and through His glorious resurrection.

This movement calls its followers to spread its message to all people, to every tribe and tongue. And the more the adherents of the movement do just that, the more it resembles the very ideal given in the pages of Scripture.

There is a growing awareness that young people not only can be a part of movements that matter, they can in fact lead them. We will not captivate this generation by patting them on the head and telling them to love Jesus a little more today than yesterday. But offer them a movement calling for absolute surrender, and they will give heed.

If given a chance. If given some guidance. If going in faith.

I join an increasing number of student pastors, researchers, parents, and especially a growing phalanx of young adults who desire to see a movement of God among students today. A movement advances before us focusing on the gospel. A shift is happening from expecting superficiality to the exposition of Scripture, from seeing youth as goofy adolescents to recognizing their ability to accomplish remarkable things while still in their teens.

Movements begin when some, often only a few, challenge the status quo with an idea or ideas that reshape the trajectory of a given group of people. Movements of God challenge the lethargy, or legalism, or liberalism of Christ followers, calling them to a radical shift in obedience and focus. The Western church has become bogged down in institutionalism, in programs, and in a minimalist approach to the Christian life.

Students in our churches too often are underchallenged and overprotected. The call to follow Christ is as radical today as it was in the first century! A wind is stirring. Student pastors, parents, and other leaders recognize the need for change. As a friend of mine once said, "When God begins to blow the wind of His Spirit, it is our job to set the sails." There is in fact a refreshing new movement of the Spirit focused on the heart of our faith. Student ministry could miss this if we don't play a few less video games and get our heads back in the Scripture.

# THE MILLENNIAL GENERATION: READY FOR A MOVEMENT

The Millennial generation offers more hope than any in a long time. They are the most educated generation in history. They are also the most studied. Just google "Millennials" and note the number of books about them. The marks of this generation offer hope, yet demonstrate the sobering reality of our inability to captivate them. While nailing down basic characteristics of a generation so vast and diverse is about like herding cats, I want to offer a few obvious marks of Millennials.

First, Millennials are *positive about the future*. From the earliest studies of Millennials by Neil Howe and William Strauss to recent authors like Thom and Jess Rainer, the hopefulness of this generation stands out.[4] Studies consistently show this generation to be positive about the future. If we can harness this optimism with a gospel vision, much could be done for the kingdom.

Next, they demonstrate a *relational* yearning.[5] I have noticed after preaching to thousands of this generation how fatherless they are. They long for real community. Social media has given the added space for online community, but they long for depth in relationships as well. They love their families, even if they have become blended or dysfunctional. They want healthy relationships in the workplace or at school. I actually teach about friendship with students today and find that students yearn to develop deep friendships. Unfortunately the church too often relegates discussions with students on relationships only to dating. We should also encourage good, godly friendships and help students who love Jesus learn to be friends of sinners, as Christ was.

This generation is *marked by learning*. Education matters to this group. I have observed this anecdotally in the numbers of student pastors who did not take seriously their own formal education and now are being pushed by Millennials they lead to be more serious about learning.[6]

I could list many other characteristics, like their connection to their parents (many of whom overprotect their children) or their connection to social media (to be discussed later). But two characteristics stand out as they relate to a missional movement.

This generation *seeks genuine spirituality and has little taste for status quo Christianity.* In his significant book *The Next Christians*, Gabe Lyons recognizes a growing movement of young believers he calls "Restorers" who "exhibit the mind-set, the humility, and commitment that seem destined to rejuvenate the momentum of the faith." These "next Christians" think and live like missionaries, not detaching the verbal presentation of the gospel from the rest of life: "Telling others about Jesus is important, but conversion isn't their only motive." He adds, "Their mission is to infuse the world with beauty, grace, justice, and love."[7]

Even experts outside the Christian world recognize the missionary nature of this coming generation. Note the findings of a magna cum laude graduate of Harvard who writes for the *Wall Street Journal*, *Boston Globe*, and the *New York Times*, among others, and calls the generation of religiously focused collegians today the "missionary generation." Referring to the 1.3 million graduates of the more than seven hundred religious colleges (not only Christian schools), Naomi Riley observes in *God on the Quad* a generation standing out from other students, quite distinctive from their secular counterparts. "They don't spend their college years experimenting with sex or drugs," she writes. "They marry early and plan ahead for family life. . . . They are also becoming lawyers, doctors, politicians, college professors, businessmen, psychologists, accountants, and philanthropists in the cultural and political centers of the country."[8]

Lauren Sandler spent over a year living among various groups of Christian young people. "I call this population of fierce young Evangelicals the Disciple Generation," she wrote, noting like Lyons how this group is "equally obsessed with Christ and with culture as a means to an Evangelical end."[9] Although not a follower of Christ, she made this staggering prediction: "It seems to me that the growth of the Disciple Generation, a movement of staggering demographic diversity united by an intensely shared faith, suggests we've arrived at a significant precipice. We are poised before the next Great Awakening in American history."[10]

> Lauren Sandler on the zeal of young adults and their potential to bring about change: "[Young people] want to reverse the flow of a river, not change its course. To reach a nation, a population needs to be redirected away from old institutions toward a radical new culture. An awakening entails young people reinventing traditional rituals, making the faith of their forefathers their own. This isn't just an observation on the MTV age – it's been the final stage of every awakening before a national transformation is complete. To hit critical mass, it takes a youth movement."[11]

A missional movement will do more than try to alter the behavior of young people and get them to show up at churches and events. It will offer a compelling opportunity to be part of God's mission through the gospel. The gospel does more than meet felt needs; it meets actual needs. Sandler observed the two things this generation seeks above all else: "Hand in hand with certainty, agape is what this generation longs for today—a love that will soothe the pain of breakups and breakouts, heal the wounds from shattered families."[12]

I find it remarkable that a recognized researcher who has no bias in favor of Christianity sees such amazing potential in this generation. I totally agree.

So much more could be said about this generation, but I will note just one more thing: their *passion for social justice and social issues.* Study the history of great spiritual awakenings and you see a consistent reality: As the gospel is recovered and proclaimed and lives are changed, the love for Christ seen in believers extends to the broken places in society. This is a generation hungry for social justice, or at the very least enamored by the idea.

We have to remind students that social justice flows from the gospel and does not serve as a replacement for it, but this impulse in Millennials offers a great opportunity for gospel work in lives and culture.

In January of 2012, more than 45,000 young people gathered in Atlanta for Passion 2012. A major theme of that gathering was human trafficking. This issue, along with adoption, poverty, and other issues, galvanized many students. Yes, we must be careful to see that the gospel stays at the forefront of social concern in the lives of these young believers. But would we not be wise leaders to take the inherent enthusiasm of youth, combined with a penchant for justice and the power of the gospel, and channel this into a movement of gospel advance? Just this week I got an e-mail from a student who attended a weekend retreat I spoke at, and he mentioned sharing Christ more than ever. He told me how his family stopped to help a homeless man and told him about Jesus. It is a massive understatement to note that this is a good thing.

One example of social justice on a simple level involves nothing more than buying a pair of shoes. This has become a big deal to our daughter Hannah. Hannah and I go to breakfast a lot and have done so from her early years as a child. One day we ate at an IHOP that happens to be in a strip mall that includes a skateboarding store. This store also sells TOMS, the cloth shoes you wear with no socks that are so ugly they are almost cute. Here is why Hannah and our son Josh and many other Millennials I know love TOMS: When you buy a pair, they donate a pair to a child who has no shoes. Hannah has multiple pairs and displays her TOMS banner proudly on her car. She had me buy a pair for myself, but at my age I prefer to wear mine with socks.

If you want to know this generation, start by looking at their shoes. TOMS shoes illustrate a vital link to understanding Millennials: They are about giving to help those in need.

Student pastors interested in getting the gospel to their community will tell you stories of meeting needs in order to share Christ. Talk to a group of teenagers in your church and, unless your youth group is still the old-fashioned, stereotypical games-driven crowd interested only in themselves, you will find some who are burdened for a friend who is a cutter or for a cause like child poverty.

The TOMS trend has far less to do with shoe styles and more to do with compassion. Inside our churches a growing number of Millennial youth keep the gospel tied to caring for people (see Acts 2:42-47). Don't get too nervous; Jesus did a lot of that as well. So did the early church. And the great awakenings did too: Whitefield not only preached the gospel in the First Great Awakening, he also started an orphanage in Savannah, Georgia, . . . in the 1700s. And it is still operating as a boys' residential school today. The gospel drives the engine of social justice. "Evangelism is the most basic and radical ministry possible to a human being," Timothy Keller has observed. "This is true not because the spiritual is more important than the physical, but because the eternal is more important than the temporal."[13]

Yes, much of Millennial fascination with helping others is superficial and trendy, just like too much of what we do in the church. But make no mistake; if you want to understand this generation, you need to be aware of the causes for which they care.

The simple example of TOMS offers a different glimpse into the spiritual commitments of students today. I am actually more excited than I have been in a long time because of this generation.

## ADVANCING A MOVEMENT OVER MAINTAINING OUR INSTITUTIONS

Although Millennials love movements and can be captivated by an understanding of Christianity more as a movement to advance than an institution to maintain, let's not forget that institutions matter. And let's help students see this. God gave us institutions: the home, the state, and the local church. I teach at an institution of higher learning. But institutions simply give boundaries to the raging river of God's movement so it does not wander off into heresy that drowns its adherents in doubt on the one hand or deadly legalism on the other.

I have been married more than thirty years. I thank God for the institution of marriage. But I never think of marriage as simply an institution to preserve; I think of it as a covenant with my wife and God through the gospel—a growing, moving relationship guided by the boundaries of Scripture. We are simply not the same people we were when we first married; we have grown and matured, and we have seen God move.

Unfortunately, in the Western church, the tendency has been to focus more on buildings, services, and programs than on lifestyle, mission, and passion. In the history of the church, you can see ebb and flow as the church moves first toward institutionalism and stagnation, then finds a fresh passion for the gospel and a renewed focus on advancing the church and the good news we have to share. Distinct waves throughout history have changed the landscape of church culture.

On a cold Halloween night long ago, a lone figure walked along the path near the Elbe River in what is now Germany. As he neared the door of the Castle Church, parchment in hand, he knew his action in the coming moments would cause a stir. But he certainly could not have imagined the impact of the movement he was about to advance. Weary of the institutionalism and failed theological views of the established church of his day, this young man had seen enough. He had written what became the manifesto of the movement soon to be called the Protestant Reformation.

The young monk's name? Martin Luther. His document? The Ninety-Five Theses. And his movement literally changed the world.

Many besides Luther had problems with the church of his day. But his theses proved to be the match that set ablaze a movement for the gospel of Jesus Christ, a movement that would go through various phases—John Calvin in Geneva, the Anabaptists and the Radical Reformation, and Zwingli, to name a few.

It is one thing to sense the need for change. It is another to be able to state what and how change should come. For a movement to captivate others who will join in spreading its message, clarity is essential.

Luther was able to both see the need for a movement and clarify a vision to accomplish it. And again today we need both—a gospel-centered movement led by those who can teach others how to effectively advance that movement.

The point, after all, is not a movement but the gospel of Christ and helping others live lives that bring glory to our great God. Movements can get in the way of that if we fail to keep the center of the movement clearly in view.

Something I have learned from speaking to and interacting with thousands of high school and college students over the past few years is this: One of the hindrances to students living relentlessly for Christ is not personal sin (although that is an issue for plenty!), but their larger perspective on the faith. Before most who grow up in our churches finish high school they have already been co-opted to a view of Christianity focused more on maintaining institutions than advancing a movement. The natural corollary to that idea is that of Moralistic Therapeutic Deism mentioned already. Institutions focus mainly on behavior, while movements focus on impact.

The reason many students seem bored with Christianity stems less from our inability to compete with the cool church down the road (or the world) and more from capturing the imagination of students with the message and mission of God. So students, who make decisions about how they will be making decisions the rest of their lives while in their teens, will fail in vital decisions again and again if they do not see Christianity as the overarching passion of life and live with a gospel-centered focus on advancing a movement.

Imagine if a teenager with his whole life ahead of him woke up every day thinking, *Today I have to act morally, be good, and make sure I get to church Sunday.*

Now imagine what a difference it would make if a teenager started her day with this thought: *Today, in some way, I get to advance the movement of God in this world. In some way, through word or actions, I get to demonstrate the love of this amazing God and live my life as part of something much bigger than myself.*

It would make a difference, would it not?

If someone asked you the meaning of life, how would you answer? If someone wanted you to tell what mattered more than anything else, could you articulate how the gospel makes sense of everything?

Many movements have come and gone, some of which had clear statements of belief. Marx and Engels penned *The Communist Manifesto*, and the communist movement influenced much of the world. Today, however, no matter how well articulated communism may be, the only places it is accepted are where totalitarian leaders rule with an iron fist. If the core values of a movement ultimately are shown to be wrong, the movement will ultimately fail.

But if the movement clearly speaks truth and gives a vision for living in light of that truth, it becomes an unstoppable force. When the gospel has been at the center of the faith of believers, Christianity has been such a force. This is why we must be relentless in our teaching of Christ as the heart of our faith, never losing the central focus of our mission.

We must take care to remember that the focus of our lives should not be on a movement itself, but on the Master of that movement. In Matthew 4:19, Jesus said, "Follow me, and I will make you fishers of men." He did not say follow a movement. Many have been led astray by zeal to follow a movement whose leader took them down a path of harm, from Islamic terrorism to the white supremacist movement. We must consistently, clearly articulate what our movement is and is not about.

It is about Christ. It is not about our preferences.

It is about worshipping God. It is not about a style of music.

It is about showing and telling others the gospel. It is not about our political or philosophical views.

Certainly the movement of the gospel will speak to preferences, style, and politics. But we too quickly lose sight of Jesus in our haste to pursue issues of secondary importance. We would do well to heed the words of Paul, a notable advancer of God's movement: "I press toward the mark for the prize of the high calling of God in Christ Jesus" (Philippians 3:14, KJV).

When we become followers of Christ, we become a part of that global movement. When Jesus walked the earth, He did not go after the cultural elite of His time. He called the outcasts and the ordinary. Folks like you and me are the kind of people God uses in His movement.

## STUDENTS AS LEADERS OF MOVEMENTS

Young people are not children finishing childhood; they are young adults preparing for a real world. In Scripture, we see this clearly. Over and over, we read of young people who did valiant, often remarkable things for God and His kingdom. Joseph at age seventeen faced tremendous victimization — his own brothers sold him into slavery, abandoned him, and lied to their father about his circumstances. Yet Joseph as a youth in difficult circumstances determined to serve God and became second in all of Egypt as a result. He became critical to the redemption of God's chosen people and thus remains central to the mission of God in Scripture and in the gospel. Miriam as a young lady risked her own life to look after her baby brother Moses. Samuel as a lad heard the voice of God when His voice was rare. David as a teenager killed Goliath and stood for God. As a youthful king, Josiah stood for God, and as soon as he became old enough to have full authority as king he abolished idolatry and witnessed a revival. As youths, Jeremiah and Daniel stood valiantly for God, and as a young woman, Esther risked her life for her people. We cannot honestly understand the amazing gospel, as it is seen in the great narrative of Scripture detailing the mission of God, without the role of young people at critical times.

Do not forget that Mary was a youth when she gave birth to Jesus, and our Lord declared He was to be about His Father's business as a twelve-year-old (is that what we expect of twelve-year-olds?). And Timothy, though not a teenager, led the church while only a youth. When one reads the Bible, one can see that God often used youth to fulfill His purposes. Because God is the same yesterday, today, and forever, we know He still uses young people. The question is whether or not we are preparing them and expecting as much of them as is our Lord.

This is true outside of the Bible as well. Young people have been remarkable in making an impact. Note these few examples:

- A. H. Francke, a theology professor at the University of Halle and a leader in the Pietist movement, witnessed a revival among students through gatherings beginning in 1686 at the University of Leipzig when he was only twenty-three.
- At age twenty-seven, Nikolaus von Zinzendorf witnessed the birth of the hundred-year Moravian Prayer Revival in 1727, which led a remarkable percentage of Moravians to leave all for foreign missions. His passion for God became obvious in his teens.
- George Whitefield launched what some have called the greatest single evangelistic tour in New England's history beginning in 1739. This was near the height of the First Great Awakening, and he was only twenty-five.
- In 1904, Evan Roberts, at age twenty-five, was a catalyst in the Welsh Revival; his lifelong focus on revival began when he was fourteen.

What if we treated men like Jim Elliot or William Carey not as the one-in-a-million exceptional Christian (so we do not have to be like them) but instead as examples of what every follower of Christ should be? We focus on these men as great moral examples, when the truth is they struggled with sin just like you and me. The greatness of their ministry was in the work of God in and through them. What if we treated every student in our student ministries and churches as a missionary with the potential to change the world for Christ? What if students and student ministries marked by such words as incarnational, intentional, and missional were the rule rather than the exception? Good news: More and more students are making this exception the new rule. Like Amy:

> My name is Amy. Mine is a story of an introverted, cynical young girl who, by the grace of God, was transformed by the gospel and compelled to communicate the hope of Jesus Christ throughout more than twenty-five nations across the globe. My story begins as an awkward eleven-year-old girl whose faith was evidenced only by my hurried mealtime prayers. When my dad announced that the family would take a two-week mission trip to work with Middle Eastern refugees in Italy, my appetite for adventure excited me about the trip. However, I didn't care much about being on mission because I didn't care much about the gospel. That is, until my eyes were opened to the gospel at work. I watched God work among their hearts and lead them to the knowledge of the truth.
>
> Since then, I have been compelled to spread the gospel, locally, nationally, and internationally. For three years I spent the entirety of my summers in South America, the Middle East, and Balkan Europe to see if, maybe, I could learn what missions really means.
>
> I didn't come away from these assignments with a new definition of evangelism or a decision to spend my life on mission in any particular place with any certain people group. In fact, I learned that I'm not a very good missionary. But I also learned to live on mission anyway.
>
> I live on mission because I have seen the goodness of God at work among the nations. I have seen Him bring hope to the eyes of an elderly woman in the former Soviet Union; rescue a young Muslim woman from guilt and shame in the Middle East; and take my stubborn, prideful heart, transform it daily, and give it a purpose far greater than I could fabricate for myself. That is a God worth living for. Even so, I am not convinced that a missional lifestyle can be boiled down to an evangelism method or a recited prayer. Though each can be a helpful tool, the most important method for me is availability. No matter where I am or how my platform is defined, the

simple act of being here, with a heart committed to God's mission and sensitive to His voice, positions me in the midst of His work.

Today, I am a full-time student with a full-time job in Alabama. But my life is not less missional because my location is less exotic. I know that I am not called to a people, to a place, or to a method, but to obedience. And I know that we are simply here to guide others along the journey of which He is the reward.

Living missionally is about being available. It's about taking advantage of every opportunity, big and small, to point another toward knowing Jesus. It's about investing in people, even those with whom you wouldn't normally spend time. It's about loving them enough to let the Holy Spirit guide your conversations into matters of eternity, about praying earnestly on their behalf, and patiently letting Him draw them to Himself through your reflection of His character, regardless of how long it may take. Ultimately, living missionally is about pursuing the heart of God as relentlessly as He pursues ours.

I guess you could call me a missionary, but in reality, I'm just a young woman who can't forfeit the opportunity for Christ to be made known through me rather than despite of me. Indeed, the hope I have received is far too great to withhold.

Sometimes we look around at our world and become pessimistic. But stories like Amy's give us hope that God is still at work! If I have any sense of what a movement of God looks like, I believe we are seeing signs of the work of God in our time. There is a growing dissatisfaction with the way things are. There is more healthy talk about the gospel, about both getting the gospel right and getting the gospel out, than I can recall. There is a rising hunger for the nations and for our neighbors. There is a rising tide of interest in church planting in the U.S., especially in cities. There is a remarkable yearning by pastors to see established churches change dramatically to refocus on the gospel.

## REVIEW AND APPLICATION

- Have you seen Christianity primarily as a movement to advance or as an institution to maintain? What difference does it make which we choose?
- Can you see students today being open to a fresh movement of God?
- Do you know any students in your church or ministry who seek to be used by God in a movement that matters? How can you help them?
- In Acts 11:19-26 we read of a missional movement that launched a church in Antioch with first-generation believers. Can you see how the Millennial generation could be part of such a movement today?

CHAPTER 4

# MISSIONAL CHURCH

### Birmingham, Alabama

The Heart of Dixie, the Buckle of the Bible Belt, and the city of my birth. Journey with me back in time to Birmingham circa 1975. My dad worked for decades as a foreman at one of the steel mills Birmingham was known for then. The generation born before 1946, those called Builders and dubbed the Greatest Generation by Tom Brokaw, built much of America by working in factories and businesses involving some form of mass production. Punch-card machines greeted workers as they entered and left the plant, and a lowest-common-denominator approach to human resources led to the rise of unions. Don't hear me describing such jobs in a negative way. This has been a noble way of life, and my dad's job helped put my brother and me through college.

You know the drill in a factory worker's world: Punch in to report to work, do your job, and go home. You could have a variety of worldviews or political views and geographic locations from which the workers came. The small town where everyone knew one another was replaced by the urbanization of the industrial revolution. Jobs were done and done well, but fewer and fewer friendships were formed at work. These and other factors fostered a minimalist approach to the job, where one did what was expected but for the most part nothing more. This created over time a love not for the value of work, but for the weekend, for vacation, and ultimately for retirement. And now my generation, the baby boomers, have a lower view of work and a higher view of leisure than the generations before us. Are we surprised at the corresponding rise in prolonged adolescence and far too many immature young men? Should we be amazed that the average video game purchaser is a thirty-five-year-old man?[1] These facts are not unconnected.[2]

Like the leaven Jesus said to avoid, a minimalistic, factory mind-set has permeated the American church. Christianity refers to those who live by faith, not those who gather in a building. But to many Americans, Christianity has become, like the factory, a path-of-least resistance, do-the-minimum part of life. Go to church Sunday. Compartmentalize, and live for those times when you have control over your leisure. Serving Christ in this context becomes more duty than delight, like the job we want to escape whenever we can.

Perhaps this explains why pastors and student pastors alike complain of apathy as a fundamental problem in the church today. Maybe this is why — out of a genuine desire to bring life to our ministries and miss the factory mind-set that perpetuates a bored congregation — many student ministries give in to sensationalism and silliness. Perhaps the very way we do things fuels the apathy we long to prevent.

Jesus has been lost in a religious system more intent on getting people to a building a minimal number of times rather than getting them to be His people on mission 24-7. No wonder we have a new category, the *dechurched*, to refer to those who grew up involved in church but never got the gospel and want nothing to do with it as adults.

To many students, following Christ seems more like punching in and doing their duty than giving their life to advance a movement. Welcome to life in the predictable church. You know the drill. Get up Sunday morning and put on those clothes. Get that Bible. Be sweet. Okay, let's be honest: The most likely time for a family to get into a tizzy is Sunday morning, true?

You show up at the church building, five minutes late of course, because nothing starts on time except for things that matter, like work or school. If you do come early or hang around after, it is probably to see friends rather than to meet with God. Sunday school is rolling soon and . . . you know the drill. Don't get too carried away. Don't challenge the teacher. Just listen passively and answer questions with the safest path-of-least-resistance answers. In other words, do not take this too seriously. Head to the service. Sing loudly. Stand up, sit down, shake hands, laugh appropriately, pay attention, nod occasionally, shake the pastor's hand, offer the obligatory "Good sermon, Preacher," beat the other church people to lunch.

Oh, and do not forget the last part of the drill, the part you really long for, because it represents leisure: Sunday nap and/or the NFL.

Okay, maybe it is not that bad. Certainly the Bible teaches that things should be done in an orderly way. And I do not want to give one more excuse for the individualism that plagues our churches and our culture. We as Christ followers are part of something bigger than ourselves, the church of the Lord Jesus Christ! But as someone who spends a lot of time with young people, and some time with the unchurched, the very predictability of what we do sometimes causes us to miss a mysterious God. Read the book of Acts—there was consistency in the early church's message and character, but one could hardly call their lives predictable.

 The church is not a hotel for saints; it is a hospital for sinners.

Church has far less to do with a building and a set time to meet and far more to do with joining other believers to serve the God who is on mission in His world. This is why seeing a new believer brings such joy. No factory mentality. No punch card. Just passion. We need a fresh touch of God to break us free from an institutional, factory mind-set and restore the joy of our salvation, giving us a passion for the mission.

## THE CHURCH: A BODY, NOT A FACTORY

When you think of the word *church*, what do you picture? Do you envision a building with a white steeple, or do you see people? The church is not a building! If every church building in our nation burned to the ground tonight, the church would still wake up tomorrow. I am not advocating the burning of church buildings, but I want to remind you that the church is less a building to attend than a people with whom we enjoy serving God. Church attendance matters, but attendance is the result of the gospel. It is not the gospel. Have we allowed the church to become a place more than a passion?

A local church is a group of believers in Jesus Christ who covenant together to serve Him as a family of faith in a given community. Your church family should be as precious to you as your blood family. We should love gathering together for regular worship, teaching, and fellowship because we love our family!

It's time to chuck the punch cards and embrace a new vision. For many today a "great Christian" has three marks: show up, serve, and be a steward. As long as you are active at the church building and you serve in some way and give money, you are a great Christian. Now, a believer who walks by faith will be active in a local fellowship and will give both time and treasure to the cause. But the minimalist approach encourages people to live for God just by giving more, showing up more, and serving more. Over time it produces people who are broke, exhausted, and never have time to connect with the lost world around them. It leads to frustration more than faith.

The church in America stands at a crossroads, and student ministry sits right in the center of the intersection. We have moved from a modern world to a postmodern context, from a world shaped much by biblical influence to a world ignorant of the Scriptures. And in the church, we too often focus on the number of students at the last event instead of the impact we are making in the local public school.

Students today yearn for something real, something compelling.

They want and need more than a factory.

The check-in, do-as-little-as-possible, check-out approach to work created in a forty-hour work week separated from the rest of life has not been compelling to the coming generation. In fact, many business books on the Millennials grapple with this generation's changing attitude toward work and life. Studies show Millennials will choose a job that matters with less pay over a better-paying job a monkey could do. In their book *The M-Factor* authors Lynne Lancaster and David Stillman identify seven aspects of Millennials: the role of parents, a sense of entitlement, a search for meaning, great expectations, the need for speed, social networking, and collaboration. "Millennials want to earn a good living while doing work that has value, whether this means contributing to a company, country, cause, or community."[3]

If the Christianity we demonstrate (because much is caught more than taught) shows our faith to be more or less a place we check into on Sundays and do the minimum so we can go about our own little lives, no wonder we have a generation of dechurched young adults.

But if we can show this generation no cause is greater than the gospel, and how the gospel through the church meets real needs in a real world, we may recapture a generation.

Theologian Jürgen Moltmann reminded us of the need to refocus our view of church: "[It] is not that the church 'has' a mission, but the very reverse: that the mission of Christ creates its own church."[4] The church does not have a mission; the mission of God has a church! Francis DuBose, whose book *God Who Sends* introduced the term "missional," said the church is "a people, a community, the people of the apostolate and a missional community. . . . More definitely, the church is the instrument of mission."[5]

▶ "The missional church believes it is God who is on mission and that we are to join *him* in it." – Reggie McNeal[6]

How will we reach a younger generation? By showing them how they were created to worship and follow Jesus. By helping them see that the gospel compels them to view the world less as consumers and more as missionaries. By showing and telling the greatness of the gospel and its effect on all of life in place of a checklist Christianity.

In another day and generation, a group of young men gathered while in college to push one another toward godliness. Weary of the status quo institutionalism of their time, they added to their studies (that had to be from God!), ministered in prisons, and fasted weekly. Ridiculed by their peers, these men ultimately led a movement of God that changed their generation.

I am talking about George Whitefield, John and Charles Wesley, and others in the Holy Club at Oxford in the 1700s. They led an awakening that shook England. I believe our current youth generation can lead a movement as well. But not if we spend more time getting them to adopt the status quo than getting them to Jesus.

## STUDENT MINISTRY: LOCAL CHURCH NOT PARACHURCH

Developing a gospel-centered, missionally driven student ministry in the personal lives of believers and in their local communities of faith is the need of the hour. It will require a healthy, robust view of the church. Pastor Mark Driscoll has noted the danger of an unbalanced focus:

Church + gospel − culture = fundamentalism

Church + culture − gospel = liberalism

Gospel + culture − church = parachurch[7]

We need all three: a love for the gospel, an awareness of culture, and a devotion for the church. This must be instilled in students if they are to become missional in their focus.

Many student ministries function as a parachurch ministry that simply meets at the local church. One complaint I hear from student pastors is that they have a huge Wednesday night attendance but much less on Sunday morning. In discussions with student pastors, it becomes evident that the reason for this is an overzealous focus on the Wednesday night "youth time" and a lack of championing of Sunday corporate worship with the whole body of Christ.

I still hear an occasional student pastor refer to Sunday morning worship as "big church." This makes students sound like little kids going to children's church who must also attend "big church." It also diminishes the relevance of Sundays to students. I understand, I really do, that far too many churches have worship services on Sunday that have little or nothing to do with young people. But we are not helping young people grow into maturity when we add to the dichotomy between a weekly time of worship for students and the time when all the people of God gather to worship the holy God and then scatter to live out the mission of God. What can a student pastor do about this?

First, you as a leader—whether a student pastor, volunteer, or parent—must **develop a love for the body of Christ as a family**, not an institution. Remember that we tend to overvalue our words and undervalue our example and the way we structure our ministries in terms of their impact on students. They need to hear from you how vital corporate worship is, and they need to see you actively participating. And they need to hear you week after week celebrating worship and, if you have it on Sunday mornings, Bible study. Remind students that God has given us two families: the nuclear family and our church family. Given that so many students come from difficult and broken families at home, we must magnify the local church more, not less.

Teach a biblical ecclesiology to your students. Too many student pastors do not have a clear doctrine of the church. You do not have to stand before students and recite to them a systematic theology of the church. But you can and must teach them basic biblical principles. To many students, the church is a man-made institution, but the church is the plan of God for the people of God to reach the world for Christ.

It is an institution, but it is more—it is the place where the movement of God should be kept before the people.

▶ Food for thought: Can your most active students articulate in a few sentences what the church is and why it matters? Will they learn it from and see it in you? Remember, students learning trigonometry in high school can handle theology in church.

Second, **at least once each year ask your pastor to speak to the students** at your student worship time. Talk with your pastor afterward about how you can bridge the gap, often very large, between worship at the designated student time and the churchwide worship experience on Sundays. By the way, that will not mean playing a game Sunday morning. If you work with students, you are part of the local church, not just a student ministry. If you are a student pastor, you serve with and are under the authority of the pastor.

Jimmy Scroggins was a student pastor for many years before becoming a senior pastor at First Baptist Church, West Palm Beach, Florida. He reminded our seminary students of the three things most of the effective pastors he knows want from a student pastor. First, he wants parents to not be beating down his door with problems. Be involved in families and be helping them. Second, most pastors are interested in attendance on Sunday morning more than any other time. As previously stated, we do not confuse church attendance on Sunday morning with being a disciple. At the same time, a follower of Christ will value that weekly time when the people of God gather to worship God. That matters more than the youth service. Corporate worship is a by-product of discipleship and can contribute to it as well. Finally, if the pastor has children in the student ministry, he wants to be sure they are being cared for. While these expectations may not represent the top list of missional markers, they serve to illustrate the reality that you as a student pastor serve with, and under the authority of, your pastor. From my years of working with student pastors and senior pastors, these represent reality and remind us that student pastors seeking to develop a missional student ministry must do so within their given context. You can accomplish your goals and be a team player.

A third way to elevate the role of the church in students is to **remind students that worshipping God is about God, not them**. Therefore the goal of corporate worship is not to make students happy but to help them become holy. Sunday morning worship with all the church should definitely not pander to students (or any other group in the church). Teach students the theological meaning and significance of worship. Theological and biblical foundations are essential to missional student ministry. At the same time, the pastor and others who prepare the gathered time of worship on Sundays should not do so as if no one under the age of twenty matters.

Fourth, **remember the goal is not to create an effective parachurch ministry for students that meets on the property of a local church**. The scorecard cannot be simply how many show up at your student worship time. Or your events. Let me be clear: Events are not in themselves evil, nor should they be abandoned. Students profit from a gathering of peers to focus on worshipping God, provided that is the focus rather than the silliness often accepted as axiomatic in student events. But events must be tied to the larger purposes of God, the local church, and then the student ministry. Events can help teach the importance of biblical doctrines like the church. But they should never be an end in themselves. Nor is the goal to create cultural, factory-driven Christians who see the goal as church attendance. The goal is to build Christ's church. Missional students will love the church as the vital family they need to help them to faith maturity and to give them accountability and encouragement. Being missional means being a self-feeder, and teaching students to feed themselves in the context of the local church will give them confidence and ability.

▶ "To treat adolescents as a separate species instead of as less experienced members of our own was one of the twentieth century's largest category errors." – Kenda Creasy Dean[8]

In Matthew 16, Jesus made it very clear that the church would stand squarely in the middle of God's plan (see verses 18-19). Read Acts 2 and see how the church was birthed and became the primary means of advancing the gospel across the world.

It still is.

The church that loses its passion for evangelism—and that is the first thing a church will lose—will also lose the younger generation. At the core of a missional church is the idea of being sent. Dean noted,

> This is the root of the church's missionary identity. Etymologically, a missionary is one who is "sent," especially one who is sent across boundaries—which makes God the original missionary, crossing every human boundary imaginable in the Incarnation of Jesus Christ. Mission originates in God, not in a church committee. The *missio dei* is God's sending of God's own self into creation, making God both the sender and the one who is sent. A church that fails to respond to the Holy Spirit's boundary-crossing impulse, that fails to share the love of Jesus—Christ God's own self in the world—is unthinkable.[9]

This is why getting a clear, missional, gospel-driven vision of Christianity matters so much. If we demonstrate to students that a church is something more akin to joining a club (and not a very exciting one from the perspective of students), we may actually hinder them from seeing Christ the more they attend our services. Dean would agree: "If churches practice Moralistic Therapeutic Deism in the name of Christianity, then getting teenagers to come to church more often is not the solution (conceivably, it could make things worse)."[10]

In their study of youth who attended Sunday school regularly throughout their teen years, Ken Ham and Britt Breemer found that 39.1 percent had become more "anti-church" following their teen years, while 26.9 percent had not become more "anti-church." Their conclusion: "The results show that Sunday school is having an overall *negative* impact on beliefs."[11] If your goal is only getting students to the church building, you may be missing the point.

Dave Kinnaman's recent book *You Lost Me* offers another sobering look at the status quo of the church. Based on an extensive survey, Kinnaman notes six primary factors for students disconnecting from church. Devoting a chapter to each, he summarizes the six as (1) overprotective toward youth; (2) shallow in their teaching aimed at students; (3) antiscience (just saying "evolution is dumb" will not cut it with this generation); (4) repressive (churches appear simplistic and judgmental on issues of sexuality, that is, young people want more than "just say no"); (5) exclusive (we need to clearly explain the exclusivity of the church—we cannot just say, "Jesus is the only way"; we must help them see why); (6) doubtless (churches seem unfriendly to those who doubt).[12] I encounter these sentiments regularly in youth and college students. We must take the timeless gospel and apply it in a timely way to deal with issues such as these. We cannot simply assume young people will embrace the faith because we said to do so or because we have embraced it.

## CHANGING DISCIPLESHIP IN THE CHURCH

While students must have a healthy understanding of the church, the church must also have a healthy understanding of where she sits in a given culture and of effective, biblical discipleship. In focusing on the lowest common denominator—trying to do generic teaching that will appeal to all students as a group—the factory-driven, institutional church gives high priority to using classrooms and curricula to create disciples. For too long many have seen discipleship as happening through the pulpit and through programs. Let the pastor (and student pastor) preach the Word faithfully and get enough people into enough classes with enough resources, and disciples will be created like a Ford assembly line.

That simply has not happened. I don't want to diminish the vital roles of faithful preaching and classroom teaching. These are essential for training if they stay focused on the gospel and mission of God. But I would argue that these general, large-scale approaches miss the personal, communal, experiential aspects of discipleship. "We must change our ideas of what it means to develop a disciple," Reggie McNeal argues, "shifting the emphasis from studying Jesus and all things spiritual in an environment protected from the world to following Jesus into the world to join him in his redemptive mission."[13]

An example of a student whose church helped her understand this is Emma. Emma's church focuses on reaching their "community, commonwealth (of Kentucky), country, and continents." Out of this vision Emma, a senior in high school, believes God has called her to serve Him overseas as a missionary. But she is not waiting until then. She and a friend named Elizabeth recently led their student ministry in a 30-Hour Famine (an experience promoted by World Vision) to benefit Pakistan. She leads in her local school's Fellowship of Christian Athletes. She and a few friends participate in a "Radical Experiment" group inspired by and outlined in David Platt's book *Radical*. She also spends time with her church doing street evangelism and medical work in Jamaica. Emma exemplifies what a young person can become when the local church casts a gospel-driven vision and includes students in it.

Those of us who take seriously the Great Commission recognize how Christ's charge compels us not to make converts on a superficial level but Christ followers in every area of life. This rightfully includes a healthy obedience to Jesus Christ, the head of the church, and a deep love for Christ's body, the local church. We cannot create missionaries without the church.

But we who make disciples must remember our own fallen state.

Though pure in motive, without great care we may—in the name of disciple making—focus on making those we disciple like us rather than like Jesus. True, Paul told those he discipled to follow him as he followed Christ, and there is a sense in which one of the best ways to show a disciple how to follow Christ is by demonstrating such a life. But we must be aware of our own biases as we lead others.

As we make disciples, we need to take care to be balanced and holistic in our training. All of us have personalities and passions that make us unique, but our goal in disciple making is less to note our uniqueness and more to spotlight Christ. If we are not careful, we will inadvertently push those we follow to pursue our personal passions more than Jesus. I would submit that three areas must be at the heart of our disciple making and mentoring:

- Orthodoxy, or right belief—we must affirm and guard fundamental teaching of Scripture.
- Orthopathy, or right affections—we must have a deep love for God and for others.
- Orthopraxy, or right actions—we must demonstrate our faith effectively in how we live.

In other words, we should be discipling others (and ourselves) to give glory to God through our head, our heart, and our hands. This is hinted at in Luke 2:52 where we read our Lord grew in wisdom, stature, and favor with God and man. We see this in the earliest description of life in the church in Acts 2:42-47:

- Orthodoxy: They gave themselves to the apostles' doctrine.
- Orthopathy: They were praising God and having favor with the people.
- Orthopraxy: They sold their possessions and distributed to those in need.

Here is how we must take care not to make followers of us rather than followers of Christ. We all have a tendency to favor one of these areas—doctrine, affection, or action—more than the others.

You probably know some believers who love to study doctrine or some subset of theology, from apologetics to a specific theological trend (eschatology, for instance). Sometimes folks given to such interests display a less-than-gracious capacity to relate to others or to practice their faith in the real world. And sometimes they would rather argue their theological convictions than take time to hear yours.

Others have a great heart for people and really love God, but the idea of a doctrinal study gives them chills. They have affection but do not value truth.

Then again, some just want to know how to "do" the Christian life. These are the activists, jumping from one cause to another, sometimes running over people who do not share their fondness for said cause, and often not able to articulate biblically why they have such an activist bent.

You may be given to one of these three tendencies more than others, but take care: If you focus on one in your disciple making to the neglect of the others, you are not making followers of Jesus. You are making followers of you.

Consider these formulas:

**Orthodoxy + Orthopraxy − Orthopathy = legalism.** The Pharisees were keen on preserving the truth and on doing their religious duties. But they did not love people. Modern-day Pharisees still don't.

**Orthopraxy + Orthopathy − Orthodoxy = liberalism.** You have heard the expression a "bleeding-heart liberal." Liberals love to talk about their love for people and causes, but loathe to talk about doctrine and changeless truth.

**Orthodoxy + Orthopathy − Orthopraxy = monasticism.** Monasteries seek to preserve a pure faith. They love those inside their safe walls. But their focus is on what goes on inside their sanctuary far more than what happens in the surrounding culture. I know many churches who function this way, gathering together regularly, loving their fellowship, standing on the promises while they sit on the premises of their church facility, but who do so little in their communities that if they vanished no one would notice.

We must be aware how we as individuals and churches focus on one of these to the exclusion of the others. We need balance. Not a milquetoast, generic version of each, but a bold, unashamed passion for truth, for God and people, and a burden to live out our doctrine and our affection effectively. Students need to see where they are strong and where they are weak in these areas, and student ministries must as well. Most student ministries focus primarily on affections, and then to some degree activism, but give far too little focus to doctrine. I want to dig deeply into the riches of God's Word, have a heart for my Savior and the people for whom He died that is apparent to all, and be able to live the faith in this culture in such a way that believers and unbelievers alike see there is no better way to live. Or to think. Or to love.

Understanding this not only helps us disciple those who have come to follow Christ, it can help us evangelize as well. Some people need to be shown theologically the truth of the gospel. But some also need to see and sense the great love of God for them in addition to the propositions of the gospel. Further, some need to see how our faith actually works in the real world, how following Christ affects our daily lives and decisions. The effective gospel bearer will learn to explain the gospel in such a way that one sees its truth, senses its heart, and realizes its practicality in a broken world.

Be busy making disciples. Just be busy making disciples of *Jesus*, with all of our hearts, minds, and activity. Such disciples may make people take notice. They did in the early church. And they will today.

## MENTORING MILLENNIALS TO BE MISSIONAL

One of the most notable ways the local church can help students live passionately for Jesus is actually one of the most biblical ways: through mentoring. Titus 2 tells us to have older men teach younger men and older women invest in younger women.

Jesus was the ultimate example of mentoring. How did Jesus involve people in His work? Did He change the world through events?

Jesus taught the multitudes.

He fed thousands.

He sent out seventy to witness.

But He changed the world with the Twelve. He especially poured Himself into three: Peter, James, and John. Event-driven student ministry obsesses with the crowds, but Jesus gave Himself to developing a few.

Nothing I do as a professor matters more than the mentoring I enjoy with my students. Andy had only been a believer a short time when he came to Southeastern Seminary. Young, fiery, and full of zeal, I liked him from the first day I met him. He had another feature I greatly value in students: He was hungry to learn. Teachable people make for great mentees and great leaders. Encourage your students to be FAT: faithful, available, and teachable.

I invited Andy to go with me on a trip. This is how I mentor much of the time, by taking people with me in the course of life. To me, this seems to be most like the example of Jesus.

Andy asked questions you would expect from a hungry young Christ follower. He came from a non-Christian background and wanted to focus every fiber of his life on following Christ. He knew he had much to learn and eagerly sought to grow.

I took him to Virginia for a weekend while I spoke at a church in the Tidewater area. (On the way back, we drove through a hurricane. I made him drive my car, which was good for his faith development and mine!) On Saturday morning, I got up early, as is my custom, to spend time with the Lord and then to begin working on a project.

At some point that morning, Andy sat up, looked around, and crawled out of his bed. He didn't say anything. (I am a gregarious person, but when I am focused on a project, I become antisocial.) A little later he looked at me and said, "You know, if you get up on Saturday morning instead of sleeping till noon, you can get a lot of schoolwork done."

I resisted saying, "Way to go, Captain Obvious." Andy, to that point, had been a typical young man who felt entitled to stay out all hours at night and goof off on the weekend. You know, he was one of those college students who claims to be passionate for Jesus but really just loves to hang out. I never gave him a lecture on study habits. I didn't give him an inspiring talk on how to be the next great scholar. I simply got out of bed and got after it, and he was *with* me to see it.

So much of life is caught more than taught. (Or perhaps it's better to say that so much of life is taught by being caught.) I learned more from my father and from mentors by watching than from listening, although both matter. I learned how to share Christ by going with someone and watching them. Part of your role as a leader in the local church is to disciple students, and doing so informally as I did with Andy has been terribly underrated in a factory-driven, assembly-line faith.

Andy and other students traveled with me for the next couple of years. We became so close that when I went on trips out of town in which he did not join me, Andy would go over and play with our then-young children. He took every class he could with me. In one particular class he met a young lady named Tanya. She had lost her husband, whom I had taught my first year at Southeastern, to a brain tumor. She asked me to speak at an event. I could not, but I had come to have a great deal of confidence in Andy, so I recommended him. Next thing you know, they were married, and now they have planted a vibrant church in Delaware and have a beautiful family. I am a great matchmaker when I don't know what I am doing.

Andy represents the best teaching I have ever done. The greatest reward for a teacher comes in the lives of men like Andy. As Paul said in 2 Corinthians 3:2, "You yourselves are our letter of recommendation, written on our hearts, to be known and read by all."

Who are the Andys in your life?

Paul advised Timothy, "What you have heard from me in the presence of many witnesses entrust to faithful men who will be able to teach others also" (2 Timothy 2:2). Mentoring leaders has received too little attention, while gurus of leadership become famous for rehashing principles better learned in a more personal relationship. Paul mentored Timothy, and Timothy mentored others. Such multiplication is one of the great needs of the contemporary church.

Leaders develop through both *formal* and *informal* mentoring. Formal mentoring is when a leader meets regularly with a small group or individual for teaching and accountability. My first formal mentoring proved to be invaluable. I was in college when a man named Curtis took two other students and me through intensive discipleship, Scripture memory, and witnessing. We used material produced by The Navigators which pushed me to grow. This vital experience marked me and should definitely be part of the scorecard for successful student ministry. However, what made this real was the times my mentor did things with me or the others outside our formal meeting time. That experience helped flesh out the topics we studied.

I know pastors who effectively mentor key laymen; others mentor young people who have surrendered to vocational ministry. Let me stop and ask you just now: Whom do you intentionally mentor?

I think any leader should be regularly meeting with a small group in a formal way. I have been doing this for years. But it is much easier to fake it if you are in a formal setting, to go through the motions while living differently away from the group. Institutionalizing always carries the danger of fossilizing, and in something like mentoring, which demands intimacy to be truly effective, the benefits of formal mentoring may be limited.

The second form of mentoring, informal mentoring, simply involves mentoring individuals in the regular, routine aspects of your life. Why? Informal mentoring lets people see you as you live life—how you respond to people, circumstances, and so on. But beware: It also lets them see you for who you are. If you as the mentor are better at talking than living, you will not long enjoy this relationship. But investing in young people, not as projects but as people for whom you care to see grow and flourish for a lifetime, can be one of the most fulfilling things you ever do.

In a given year, I literally spend hundreds of hours with my students by simply involving them in my daily life—going on trips, doing yard work, running errands, and so on. Some of my best teaching has come in those times, and the deepest, most lasting relationships have grown from them. (I have written an e-book called *With: A Practical Approach to Informal Mentoring* that explores this in more detail. It's available from Amazon.com.) So, do you truly want to create a missional culture in your student ministry? Connect students to the church, let them see you living a missional life, and invest in them as you go, encouraging other leaders to do likewise.

> As you go, make disciples. . . . Is that not only the Great Commission but also the great example of Jesus Christ (see Matthew 28:19-20)? A missional ministry is inseparable from a missional life.

By the way, students can mentor others as well. One of the most meaningful meals our son Josh had while in middle school came when a high school student he greatly admired in our church picked Josh up before school and took him to breakfast. Get your leaders in high school investing in middle school students. Create a culture of mentoring, and if enough of your mentors seek to live missionally, you will wake up one day and discover a shifting culture in your student ministry.

And that may just change your whole church.

## REVIEW AND APPLICATION

- How important is the local church—that is, the whole church—to your understanding of discipling students?
- Do you see instances where the church today functions more like a factory with minimal standards than as a movement costing everything?
- Read Acts 2:41-47, the earliest summary of the church. Do you sense from this passage the emphasis is on the church as an institution or on the growing lives of the believers?
- What can you do to help instill a passion for the church and a passion in your church for developing a missional, disciple-making culture?

# CHAPTER 5

# MISSIONAL LENS

## L.A.

Those initials may make you think of Los Angeles, but where I come from they stand for Lower Alabama. Not the place many think of when planning a honeymoon or exotic vacation (I am typing this while sitting on a porch in the Florida Keys, which resembles nothing I have seen of rural L.A.). But the southern part of Alabama has a very special place in my heart.

In my office, I have a framed poster from this L.A. Old, stained, and faded, the poster has seen its better days. It announces a "Youth Revival" August 2–5 at the Cubahatchee Baptist Church in Lower Alabama. The evangelist: a young kid named Alvin Reid. The year: 1981. I had just finished college, gotten engaged, and was spending the summer traveling across my home state preaching four-day youth revival meetings. The poster may not seem attractive, but to me it signifies a beautiful work of art, for it reminds me of a time when I could not believe anyone would let me preach, and how honored I was to preach to a crowd of a few dozen and a handful of teens.

For most of my life, I have been involved in itinerant ministry, preaching in more than two thousand churches, from a mission church in Montana to a megachurch in Florida. This also includes well over a hundred Disciple Now events, scores of camps, and countless youth rallies. I keep the faded old poster in my office to help me remember where I came from, to be grateful for the small rural churches that allowed an ignorant, on-fire young preacher like me into their pulpits.

## THE MISSIONARY GENERATION

Along the way, I've met interesting people, including many remarkable young people. One of the reasons I believe so much in the potential of students today comes from those I have met, so many of whom seek to live on mission with Christ. They understand the missional call much better than those who came before them, once someone takes the time to show them what that looks like. Take, for instance, my friend Morgan. I met Morgan when I spoke at her church, just as I have met so many students in so many churches. She caught me afterward to tell me about her ministry. She and her friends had started a ministry to fight the blight of human trafficking, especially the trafficking of young women as sexual slaves. You may or may not be aware of the fact that there are about 27 million people on earth today who classify as slaves, more than any other point in history.[1] At the time I met her, she and her friends had raised almost four thousand dollars to send overseas to rescue young women.

Did I mention Morgan's age? She was fourteen at the time. And the other six girls, who started the ministry with the help of their parents and their church, are all under sixteen.

Morgan gives much credit for her passion for the broken to her family and church encouraging her from the start and believing she and her friends could do great things in the name of Jesus. Morgan, Brianna, Maleah, McCall, Claire, Kristie, and Elise have joined a movement propelled by the gospel that applies the unchanging Story of God's love in our broken world today.

At age twelve, Morgan and her friends began weekly Bible study. Let her tell you the story:

Learning to dig through the Word with godly girls was an invaluable means in my life of growing closer to God. I'm so grateful for the investment that my mom and several other ladies made in our lives then to shape us into the teens that we are becoming now. Through a variety of circumstances—our church's first Global Impact Conference, a trip to India at age thirteen, and others—God continued to show me the needs of the world.

The Fourth of July, 2010, happened to be on a Sunday. In Bible Fellowship that morning my eighth grade girls' class spent time praying and thanking God for our freedom. At one point I mentioned the fact that I was grateful for not being literally enslaved in physical bondage, specifically enslaved to satisfying the sexual desires of ruthless men. I mentioned my concern for trafficked girls. A few days later, a few friends and I decided to have a sleepover. We shared about how we really wanted to do something with our high school years bigger than ourselves—something to make a difference. We began to focus on the issue of trafficked women, and the ministry of Save Our Sisters (SOS) was born. Since the birth of SOS, the Lord has blessed us with over $40,000 to set the captives free! God has been continually shaping the vision and goal of our ministry.

The following July my fellow SOS member Brianna and I were able to travel to Cahul, Moldova, often described as the engine of the sex slave trade. With a population of only 5 million, nearly 25 percent of all Moldovan women are trafficked throughout Europe. Women serve as Moldova's number one export.

During our time in Moldova, we visited a Freedom Home in the capital city of Chisnau for rescued victims of trafficking. From our first greetings with the girls, we immediately felt the love of Christ exude from their sweet spirits. These women are living out redemption stories every day.

We learned that over the past ten years, 30,000 women have been trafficked from the city of Cahul. As a ministry, SOS began pursuing the dream of building a safe home in Cahul. We are working to make this dream a reality. To help us achieve this goal, we work with Immanuel Baptist Church in Cahul, a young church planted by Christ Baptist Church in Raleigh, North Carolina.

In addition to the home, land in Cahul will also be used for an orphanage and sports camp. Sports camps serve as the main means of evangelism in the lives of Moldovan teens. Through this sports camp, we will take steps toward the prevention of trafficking. By teaching the girls the tell-tale signs of traffickers, potential victimization can be avoided. As for the orphanage, that will be a preventative step as well. By housing orphan children, the girls will be off the streets and minimize their vulnerability. Children of the orphanage and sports camp will hear the good news of the gospel and will prayerfully begin to root themselves in the love of Christ. Experiencing freedom in Christ is the most effective means of prevention, intervention, and restoration for the whole scope of the human trafficking industry. We praise God for such an awesome opportunity to serve in multiple capacities!

Morgan's involvement in this focus has helped her develop a missional lifestyle daily as well:

In being a part of SOS, God has allowed me to constantly be on mission for Him. Our first mission is to share freedom for all captives found in Christ. We are all enslaved to something in our lives. The lives of these girls provide a very literal picture of slavery. Yet if we dig a little bit deeper in our lives, we see places of bondage in each of our lives. In this way, we see that we are much like these precious little girls. Slavery masks itself in many ways, but it is slavery just the same. Freedom is here.

Students need three things from those older than them: a vision as big as the gospel, encouragement that they can serve Christ now, and permission to do so. Morgan epitomizes this. Her pastor at the time was

Al Gilbert, a man with a heart for the nations. He spoke to her and her parents about India. I have known Al for a long time, and one of the marks of his ministry has been to encourage young people to get started early going to the mission field to develop a Great Commission vision for life.

Morgan exemplifies a young person who has begun to realize that she is more than a cog in a system, that her life can matter for God. Each person has been created in the image of God and thus can uniquely honor Him and serve Him for His glory.

 Three things every student needs: a gospel vision, encouragement, and permission to live valiantly for Christ *now*.

Seth Godin argues in *Linchpin* that every person on earth in some way has genius, and how each person can be—in fact must be—remarkable. But he also observes how society tends to discourage being remarkable and encourage rote conformity:

> No one is a genius all the time. Einstein had trouble finding his house when he walked home from work every day. But all of us are geniuses sometimes. The tragedy is that society (your school, your boss, your government, your family) keeps drumming the genius part out. The problem is that our culture has engaged in a Faustian bargain, in which we trade our genius and artistry for apparent stability.[2]

Think about it: Young people hear from their earliest days to follow the rules, to comply, to obey, to fit in. And well they should. They are fallen sinners who need constantly to be reminded what is right and wrong. But in our focus on teaching these facts I fear we omit another vital part of what they need to hear, and that is to be remarkable.

Take a look at sports. We hate it when people cheat, especially when it is the opposing team. Let a ref miss an obvious pass interference play that costs your team the win and you and I are infuriated, and rightly so. But what we *really* love is when someone in the context of the rules of the game makes the unbelievable play to win the game: the buzzer beater, the goal-line stop, the miraculous catch.

We spend so much time telling young people to conform, but without also telling them that within the boundaries of God's Word they can soar. That is not at all to undermine the importance of daily faithfulness, of ordinary obedience, which God certainly uses. But far too many students today have a sense of boredom about their faith because they need a greater biblical understanding of this great God and His redemptive work, and they need to be more involved in that work in the world.

Remember the factory analogy I used in the last chapter? The person who first helped me see this is the same Seth Godin I quoted on the previous page. Read his thoughts about the American Dream and how we have failed to help people see themselves as remarkable:

> Here's the deal our parents signed us up for: Our world is filled with factories. Factories that make widgets and insurance and Web sites, factories that make movies and take care of sick people and answer the telephone. These factories need workers. If you learn how to be one of these workers, if you pay attention in school, follow instructions, show up on time, and try hard, we will take care of you. You won't have to be brilliant or creative or take big risks. We will pay you a lot of money, give you health insurance, and offer you job security. We will cherish you, or at the very least, take care of you. It's a pretty seductive bargain.[3]

Want to know why so many students who have grown up in church seem bored to death with it? Churches have, by and large, bought into the same low-risk mentality.

## STUDENTS CAN BE MISSIONARIES NOW

Patrick grew up in a fairly spiritual home. But in his sixteenth year, something tragic happened: He found himself a victim of kidnapping and a prisoner of people from another land. While captive, he remembered his mother's prayers and surrendered to Christ. He ultimately escaped while still young but felt an undeniable call to be a missionary. He did not merely have a general tug toward missions, but rather a specific calling from God to reach those who had kidnapped him.

So Patrick, now remembered as Saint Patrick, evangelized Ireland about a millennium and a half ago. He was not the first young person to take seriously a call to a missional life, nor will he be the last. What about students you know?

> You are not a missionary because of where you live. It is not based on being "far away." You are a missionary because you have a mission. That makes every follower of Christ, in every time and place, a missionary.

We have done a far better job at teaching the law than the gospel. The fact is that students who only hear behavior modification, follow the rules, or conform, miss the remarkable nature of the gospel to free us to serve our God with remarkable creativity. By failing to show the wonder of following Christ and the opportunities that brings for glorifying our King, we give further motivation for students to rebel.

When a student mostly hears "Just say no," he rarely responds with remarkable faith.

We must help young people see that the "You are just a cog in a system" idea is not affirmed anywhere in Scripture. Read the life of Abraham and Isaac, or Samuel, or David, or Josiah. They are hardly cogs in a system. I would submit that you see far more evidence of each lover of God in Scripture being marked by uniqueness than by conformity.

I met a young lady once who demonstrated this. Now in her midtwenties and following Christ, she told me she grew up in a large youth ministry. But the only two things she remembered clearly from those days were "don't have sex" and "invite a friend." Okay, that is one person's story. Or is it?

Too often what young people hear and see is something like this: Be moral. Fit in. Don't get crazy or be too loud or too different. Be like the others around you, behave, get a good job, have a nice family, and stay in church.

What if, instead, we said something like "You are remarkable" to every student, not only with words but with our lives and in how we do everything in our ministries? The majestic, awe-inspiring, Creator God made you in His image. You are like no one else. No one has your DNA or your fingerprints. God made you to worship Him and bring Him glory. The amazing thing is this: The only way for you to be the remarkable, unique, creative person God made you to be is by His grace. You cannot do it. So the amazing gospel shows us that to be creative, we have to conform—but not to society, to Christ. And the closer we draw to Him, the more we have freedom to be an agent of radical impact for Him in our world.

## EACH STUDENT CAN LIVE A UNIQUELY MISSIONAL LIFE

The lowest-common-denominator approach to student ministry—what will be most effective for the largest number of students at one time—is fine for a rally, but cannot be the basis for a ministry. Event-driven student ministry naturally leads to the lowest common denominator, because events mean crowds, and crowds always push you to the lowest point of commonality. I love how in Acts 2 we read of a modest band of believers witnessing (about 120), and then a crowd of three thousand. Then we read of a lame man healed and saved in chapter 3, and over five thousand men by chapter 4. Then we read of a single Ethiopian eunuch in Acts 8, and a single woman named Lydia in Acts 16, and others.

Throughout the narrative of Acts, we read of both massive crowds and unique individuals. The common thread is a gospel impulse that pushed believers further toward those yet unreached. We cannot lose the focus on individuals even as we gather crowds. But more than that, we need the mind, heart, and life of a missionary.

Part of "lowest-common-denominatorism" comes from the modern practice of mass production. Henry Ford developed a system of mass production for automobiles, and today we think nothing of mass production, although it is actually quite modern in practice. But while assembly lines are great for making cars, they are not God's design for turning Millennials into missionaries.

The impersonal routine of the assembly-line mentality is horrible for making disciples, yet it fills our church culture. We have too often created programs and formulas that do not so much help individual Christ followers grow in knowledge of how they can live out the gospel uniquely, but merely tell them to follow a curriculum through a class-room for a designated time. The era of disciple making by the twin methods of pulpit and program (see chapter 4) will not cut it in this generation. Yes, we must teach well and provide the best curriculum possible. But the idea that getting enough people into enough classrooms with enough curriculum to mass-produce disciples has never worked, and certainly will not now. The Morgans of this world demand more.

Just because you can mass-produce curriculum does not mean you can mass-produce disciples. But lowest-common-denominatorism leads to remarkably disinterested believers, not remarkable ones. A funda-mental aspect of being missional is to be a self-feeder, someone who can take initiative and be adaptive. The more we help students get the heart of a gospel-focused life, the more they can personally grasp how to live that life through the local church in their given community. This is the heart of disciple making. Students today already feed themselves in remarkable ways via social media and the world of Google. They can handle information, videos, Facebook, and their music; they can learn to manage the mission as well.

Certainly students are at different places and at first will need specific examples and projects to get them thinking outside the church-factory box. We will have to help a seventh grader a lot more than a senior. But if our seniors who have been with us since they were seventh graders have no clue about living the mission, that is our fault.

This is not as hard as it may seem. Help students see how their normal, daily interests, hobbies, and abilities can be used for the gospel. Help them see how anything that is not inherently evil can be used to bridge relationships in order to share Christ. Help them see that helping those around them is part of the larger witness God gives them. I have known students who led friends to Christ via sports or video games, for instance, or as they interacted online via social media.

It is time to release the hounds. It is time to help young people see how they can learn, while they are still young, to own their own faith, to discover who they are in Christ, to drink deeply from the well of the Word and step out with vigor to impact the world for Jesus.

Being missional means to think like a missionary. That requires the ability to *think*. Assembly-line Christianity teaches what to think, not how. We must teach well the foundational truths of life as a Christ follower. We must be relentless in teaching a gospel-centered worldview. But we must also do that in such a way that students can apply that truth to their individual lives as God has uniquely created them.

Our daughter Hannah left the security of a Christian school to finish high school at a large public school. Why? She wanted to make an impact for the gospel. What if we spent less time teaching on a hundred different subjects and instead taught the glory and the Story of the gospel as foundational to all things, and then helped students individually (and with their friends) think like missionaries? This is admittedly harder and takes more time. It is really not that hard to run an assembly line.

Just what does it mean to think like a missionary?

Wait. If you believe students are simply kids capable mostly of playing video games and being childish, none of the rest of this matters.

But if you believe that young men and women in their teen years can be remarkable, read on.

## MARKS OF A MISSIONAL STUDENT: THE SCIENCE

I want to look at helping students develop a missionary lens in two ways. First, let's examine the *science* of missionary thinking and living. Science is founded on basic laws such as the law of gravity. You cannot ignore basic laws in nature and get very far in science. The same is true missionally. We must build individual or group strategies on unchanging truth. By the way, if lowest-common-denominatorism works at all, this is where it does. Every student needs to get the essential message of Christianity and the mission God has for us. This should be championed at every rally, event, and activity, each Sunday, again and again. As a good football team goes over certain drills every practice, the gospel cannot be recounted too often. Much of this I developed back in chapter 1 on the subject of what is missional, but here I want to summarize a few key points:

1. *Thinking like a missionary means understanding the message of God and the mission of God* (see chapter 2). Understanding who you are in Christ, how you are free to serve Him not out of bondage but because this was the very reason you were created, how to see everything in life from the lens of the gospel, all this is vital. The great narrative of Scripture—Creation, Fall, Rescue, Restoration—teaching the redemptive love of God in Christ must be central. The more clearly the idea is seen at the heart, the more freely one can apply that idea in life and relationships.

Missional refers to a concept, not a program, posture, or skill set. "Being missional involves an active engagement with this new conversation to the point that it guides every aspect of the life of the missional believer," Reggie McNeal observes, adding,

> To think and to live missionally means seeing all life as a way to be engaged with the mission of God in the world. This missional

understanding of Christianity is undoing Christianity as a religion. The expression of the Christian movement in North America is fundamentally altering before our very eyes. The shifts are tectonic. They involve both form and content. These developments go way beyond denominational affiliations, party labels (liberal, conservative, mainline, evangelical), corporate worship styles (contemporary, traditional), program methodological approaches (purpose-driven, seeker-friendly), or even cultural stances (postmodern, emergent, emerging).[4]

2. *Thinking like a missionary means knowing what does not change* (the gospel, the Scripture, the plan of God, clear biblical teaching on topics from marriage to the church to daily life). But it also means while you hold these truths tenaciously you hold your personal preferences tentatively.

3. *Thinking like a missionary also means understanding culture and how to relate the gospel to people in a given culture.* This means we understand our role as more than merely getting people to a church building weekly. It means we seek to add value to our communities because gospel-centered lives do that.

We have to help students recognize the extremes of avoiding culture on the one hand, which leads to legalism and the Christian bubble, or being obsessed with looking like the culture on the other, which leads to worldliness. The gospel must remain central to all we do. This will not happen overnight, but it could change a generation.

A student in your ministry may not rescue a nation from famine. But a student could do something valuable in the local school that also helps to proclaim Christ. Missionaries overseas bring value by building hospitals, digging wells, and through other means. Helping students do this individually and as a student ministry can help them develop a missional lifestyle for the rest of their lives.

## MARKS OF MISSIONAL STUDENTS: THE ART

Another side of helping a student think and live missionally matters as well, and that is the *art* side. Lowest-common-denominatorism discourages artistry. I'm not referring merely to our common usage of the term, but art in the sense of something masterful or transcendent amidst the routine, something powerful, passionate, and uniquely expressive. Study the history of the church, however, and you will see a remarkable variety, an artistry if you will, to the ways God used so many different people and movements for His glory.

No one describes the need for artistry in a general sense better than Seth Godin. "A cook is not an artist. A cook follows a recipe, and he's a good cook if he follows the recipe correctly," Godin observes, adding, "A chef is an artist. She's an artist when she invents a new way of cooking or a new type of dish that creates surprise or joy."[5]

I fear we are taking a generation of chefs and turning them into cooks.

By helping students see themselves as artists, we can help them think missionally. We already do this to some extent, but we do it in extremely narrow, safe, Christian-bubble categories. When we have a talented young lady who loves to sing, we tell her to become a Christian singer. When we have a young man who is gifted athletically, we tell him to be a Christian athlete. Yet their talents and passion may be used in a variety of other ways and do not have to be confined to the "Christian" enterprises approved by the Christian subculture (see chapter 6).

We should not be telling them what to be anyway. We should be showing them Christ, that He is the Way, and helping them find their way by surrendering all to Him. As a parent, the easy thing would be to tell my children to do this or be that. The more rewarding task comes from helping them know God and His ways so they can discover for themselves the unique and personal steps leading to a life most glorifying to Him.

That, after all, is the point.

Today there is a whole new breed of young people who have taken the genre of rap and made it the most gospel-centered form of music available. Just tonight I found myself stuck in St. Louis with a delayed flight and had a two-hour conversation with Propaganda, one of the new generation of artists who use the platform of rap and spoken word to bring faith and culture together.

When a young person hits play on her iPod she probably gives no thought to Thomas Edison. But Edison invented the phonograph, which led to a revolution in recorded music, which is today dominated by downloadable and streaming music services. However, Edison did not invent the phonograph to play music; his intent was to record final words of the dying.

As Kevin Kelly observes in *What Technology Wants*, "With few exceptions technologies don't know what they want to be when they grow up."[6] He observes how a year after inventing the phonograph, Edison made a list of its possible uses; playing music was little more than an afterthought. Kelly argues rightly that the inventor of a new technology hardly ever sees its full potential, in part because he sees it only as a means to improve something, making an old thing work better. It is hard to imagine the Chinese, who invented gunpowder, immediately thought of inventing the gun to go with it.

If you work with students this could be a helpful lesson in leadership. Sometimes we who are parents or who work with students want to lay out a clear directory of options and then help them pick the most reasonable item from the directory we set before them. But what if we focused less on specific options and more on helping develop a trajectory out of which they can make decisions about their future confidently?

The inventors of new technologies, or at least those who used these advancements later, had to apply the technologies in ways originally not clear. Even Edison's "directory," the list of possible uses of the phonograph, missed its greatest potential, and Thomas Edison was one smart fellow!

What if we as parents and student pastors focused young people much more on understanding the gospel and its implications for all of life, and stepped back a bit to let them see which direction God takes them? What if that young lady who is in middle school and has a wonderful singing voice could do something more than, say, become a contemporary Christian singer? What if she had a greater ability than singing and could best use that artistic genius as a graphic designer or a creative thinker in some other venue? What if that young man who naturally leads others went to law school instead of seminary and became a champion for the disenfranchised? What if that quiet young fellow who loves tinkering with technology became the next Edison?

What if our well-intentioned attempts to help students "discover the will of God for their life" actually limited them to what we think they could do or be? What if we spent more time helping them understand the gospel is more than a vertical means to heaven, as vital as that is, but also a horizontal means to their life as part of God's mission?

This is much harder, of course, than simply naming the great Christian colleges out there or listing typical roles and pushing students toward one of those. It will take a much greater focus on discipleship than events, and a much deeper push to understand faith, culture, the gospel, and life. It actually involves both trajectory and giving a directory, for we can certainly help students with options they face, but I think we should micromanage that part less and give much more attention to a gospel, missional trajectory. Without ignoring realities, how does the gospel compel them for the sake of God's glory?

Recently I divided my students into groups, giving each a possible scenario in which someone came to them seeking help. Half the scenarios involved believers who struggled with homosexual temptation, had deep anger issues, were control freaks, and so on. Half the scenarios involved unbelievers who were in failing marriages, struggling with alcoholism, and other problems. Part of my reason for doing this was to see whether students would deal with these from a gospelcentric viewpoint and not just give general advice. Some found it hard to shift from giving three points of practical how-to (a directory) to building on gospel truth (a trajectory). But I also wanted them to see a second thing: Whether you are helping the lost or the saved, base all the help you offer on the work of Christ.

If the generation of students we lead grasps the message of God in the gospel and the mission of God to others, upon that foundation we can build wise counsel for making key decisions in the rest of life. But any wisdom we offer apart from God's mission and the gospel message will not help build a lifelong trajectory. And rather than funneling assembly-line Christians into factory-driven religion, we have the opportunity to release a generation of missional artists into the culture. They can punch in and out until ultimately retiring from active church duty to indulge comfortable preferences. Or a gospel trajectory can send them boldly into new territory, glorifying their Creator with a variety of talents.

▶ "God only had one Son, and He made Him a missionary." — David Livingstone[7]

If we really believe the Bible is not about us and our plans but about God and His purpose, we will spend less time simply giving information and experiences and more time helping students learn to think strategically and missionally. That would mean a central part of our disciple making would involve helping believing students develop a plan for their life to be missional. But they are only teenagers, right? No one actually lets teenagers develop a plan for their lives and then execute it, do they?

What if we helped students finishing high school to think about college from the perspective of where they could not only get a degree but where they could most effectively live the mission of God on campus? I speak at a lot of state universities, and one thing I say to Christian students is the number two reason they are at that campus is to earn a degree, and the first is to be a missionary. I cannot tell you how many students have come to me to thank me while also admitting they had never even thought of that. Should the mission not influence our college choice?

## THE COST OF MISSIONAL LIVING

One of the things we must be very clear about as we lead students to a missional lifestyle is the cost of discipleship. What I propose here has no resemblance to the prosperity gospel. Students serious about living for Jesus in this culture will be criticized at the very least. It may cost them friends. Even some in the church may not understand their zeal.

But the fact is most of our students have not been prepared for the real world of fallen humanity and the cost of following Christ. Making Christ and His message the center of life instead of our desires will help prepare students not only for impact but also for disappointments. As I have told my children often, life is not fair. But God is good.

In the early centuries of Christianity, the believers made a phenomenal impact for the gospel in two specific ways. The first one we know well: They stood courageously in the face of persecution. From *Fox's Book of Martyrs*, which I first read as a student, to the historical accounts of heroes like Justin Martyr, we can read of believers' boldness. Thanks to the Voice of the Martyrs and other ministries, we can be aware of the many who suffer for their faith today as well. When I take students out witnessing, I tell them that whenever someone mocks or criticizes them, they can proudly consider themselves a member of Persecution University. Of course, students in the West face nothing like many in other parts of the world. But we must help students here understand that being like Jesus means some will persecute us. Following Jesus could cost a spot on the team, a job promotion, or worse. And He is worth that and more.

When Hannah and I were in Thailand we saw a young lady named Alisa come to faith in Christ. The day after she was saved, her boyfriend beat her badly. She moved into the hotel room with Hannah and her roommate. Night after night she would read her Bible well into the night, so grateful to know God. She continues to be a great inspiration to us and to many because of her walk with Christ in the face of difficulty.

But another, more overlooked, aspect of the way the early church made an impact was the way they responded to the times of plagues. On two occasions a plague wiped out huge numbers of the population of the Roman Empire. In these times the pagan physicians would flee for their own lives. But believers stayed and ministered, even though doing so meant many of them would die of the plague themselves. Help students see how Jesus is worth risking our comfort, our plans, and our stuff for His cause.

Jesus said in Luke 9:23 we must take up our cross and follow Him, and if we will not do so we are not truly His followers. A young man named Ben certainly understood this. His is an example of a young man who faced tremendous physical hardship and used it to point others to Christ. Ben went to elementary school with my son and was a part of our church. Ben was diagnosed with ALS, or Lou Gehrig's disease, in August 2009. This incurable disease gradually takes away one's ability to function—to walk, eventually eat, until life ends. It is a horrible reminder of a fallen world.

Ben died in December of 2009. But as Ben faced this reality, he posted a testimony on YouTube to let the world know his hope in Christ was greater than the suffering he faced. (Search YouTube: "Ben McNeal—Finished Well" to experience his amazing story.) Even in his difficulty he wanted to use his life as a testimony to the gospel. "ALS is not something I have to worry about," he said. "I'm free to live my life for Jesus Christ." Ben was far more concerned with a lost person coming to know Jesus than with being delivered from his plight. "Deep down inside I just want to be a blessing," Ben said. "Having ALS has definitely caused me to see my life from another point of view. I'm not mad at God for this; what an honor and privilege it is to live for Him. I want people to see my life and wonder at Jesus. I don't have a lot of money, but I can show you there is peace in the storm."

Seeing the world as a missionary not only gives a student a positive direction for life, it gives the means to face suffering as well.

## REVIEW AND APPLICATION

- Do you often think of the potential missionary force in your student ministry? What can you do to help develop that potential?
- The statement was made that a believer is not a missionary based on where you are, but on what your mission is. How well do your students understand this? How can you help them grasp this?
- While every believer is a missionary, God does call some to specific, vocational ministry as pastors or other local church leaders, and He calls some to move across the nation or across the globe as vocational missionaries as well. Do you challenge students to consider God's call in this area?
- Read Isaiah 6:1-8. Isaiah, the godliest man in the nation, recognized his own sin. After God forgave him Isaiah was ready to go anywhere and do anything for the Lord. What can you do to challenge students to serve God no matter their location or vocation?

# CHAPTER 6

# MISSIONAL SURGERY

### Thessaloníki, Greece

In 2010, I journeyed to Thessaloníki, Greece, on a mission trip. I stood at the gate of a very old and massive wall at the edge of the city. Scripture records in Acts 17 that Paul entered ancient Thessalonica, presumably at that site, and caused more trouble than an Oklahoma tornado for the spiritual status quo of Macedonia. Paul seemed to cause a revival or a riot (or both) at every city he visited, and this was no different. Thessalonian opponents of the early Christian movement cried, "These men who have turned the world upside down have come here" (Acts 17:6).

A missional revolution among students in our time would have a similar effect.

When we turn to 1 Thessalonians, we read the first epistle written by Paul. After his greeting in 1:1-4, we read Paul's first words to the early believers in this Macedonian city. What did Paul describe? A missional movement. He reminded them how the gospel came to Thessalonica:

> Because our gospel came to you not only in word, but also in power
> and in the Holy Spirit and with full conviction. You know what kind

of men we proved to be among you for your sake. And you became imitators of us and of the Lord. . . . For they themselves report concerning us the kind of reception we had among you, and how you turned to God from idols to serve the living and true God. (verses 5-6,9)

How did the gospel come? In word (it always came in word in the New Testament), but *not* in word *only*. Power and the Holy Spirit marked their ministry. They demonstrated conviction regarding their message. And note the obvious missional feature: "You know what kind of men we proved to be among you."

But there is more. After the gospel changed the first believers in the city, we read the practical impact of the gospel on their lives: They turned from idols to serve a living and true God. Today, we still must call people to turn from idols. We need the Holy Spirit to do the work of a surgeon, regularly removing the cancer of idolatry that so easily fills our heart. Our missional focus must not only be positive, focusing on our great God and His glorious gospel; it must also keep a watchful eye for the idols our heart so quickly erects to hinder our gospel advance.

Sadly, as we ministered in modern-day Thessaloníki, we saw the ugly face of idolatry as well. This time the idolatry was seen in the dominant church there. Walking into one of the cathedrals, one can quickly see the enslavement of so many to a religious system that seems for those we observed to be virtually devoid of Christ. An elderly lady slipped a piece of paper with her burdens under the glass behind which lay the remains of a former priest. This dear lady thought this dead priest, not the living Christ, could help her. The building reeked of ritual, religion, and dead morality and was devoid of grace, hope, and intimacy with God through Christ. But it was not unlike some churches I have been to in the States, and I must admit my own heart at times confuses ritual with reality.

It is easier to see the idolatry in others than in ourselves sometimes. But we too live in an idolatrous culture.

# CONFRONTING THE IDOLS OF OUR TIME

When Paul came to Athens as recorded in Acts 17, he was struck by the idolatry in the city. The Bible speaks much about the struggle between faith in God alone and idolatry. The first two of the Ten Commandments deal directly with idolatry. If we are to help Millennials become missional, we must be honest about the hindrances to living as missionaries. Let's be clear: We are talking about a revolution for many, a new way of thinking about Christ and His church. We can't only give students the hope of the gospel and principles of missional living; we must also confront the idols that keep us from living relentlessly for Him. My mother, who turned eighty yesterday, has survived cancer thirty-eight years. Why has she survived? Because when the doctor discovered a tumor, she allowed him to remove it surgically. Hebrews 4 tells us the Bible is like a surgeon's knife, excising that which would do us harm. We need the regular, surgical removal of the idols of our heart.

Few people in recent days have written with greater clarity on our times than Tim Keller. His books have been prophetic in their elevation of the gospel and their demolition of idols. He argues American culture reeks of idolatry, noting that idolatry refers not only to obvious, blatantly false gods, but also to how an otherwise good thing can become a god thing. Sports, media, relationships, money, all these and more are not satanic in themselves, but an obsession with them turns them into false gods.

"Instead of living for God, we begin to live for ourselves, or our work, or for material goods," Keller observes, adding, "We reversed the original intended order." As a result, instead of ruling over creation as God intended, "now creation masters us."[1]

Many good things lie in the path of students today that, while not in themselves evil, may be the very issues that prevent students from relentlessly pursuing a Christ-centered life. Some of the idols may be created or promoted by the church that should be pushing them aside to reach the world.

I want to encourage you to consider the idols of our time—the idols in your church, community, student ministry, and in your heart—but to focus especially on those that specifically stop the missional impulse from growing in our hearts and ministries. What keeps me from living for the glory and the Story of God? What hinders me from investing in a lost world? Security and comfort, for instance, neither of which are in themselves bad things, can become idols if my love for security and comfort prevents me from sacrificing my time, my talent, and my treasure for the sake of the gospel.

The following offers a sampling of some good things that can become idols, cutting the cord of missional Christianity.

## THE IDOL OF CONSUMERISM

Want to attend a worship service? You don't have to go to a church building. Go to a shopping mall. Modern malls are built with principles gained from great cathedrals with their massive spaces and impressive architecture. You enter and see a map to guide the worshippers of materialism who gather from all across the region. You look up to see windows overhead giving "a sense of vertical and transcendent openness that at the same time shuts off the clamor and the distractions of the horizontal, mundane world,"[2] James K. A. Smith observes. They are intended to give a sense of awe and to provide a multiplicity of opportunities to "worship." The massive windows filled with items of our consumption demonstrate a truly good life, encouraging us to participate with others in celebrating our personal fulfillment in our devotion to material possessions. Smith notes in great detail the way shopping malls compel us not at the level of base greed, but by tugging at the cords of our yearning to worship.

Consumerism has become a god in our time, and the shopping mall our cathedral. The religion of the American Dream has invited us to partake of the fruit of personal satisfaction in the form of stuff. "This temple," Smith writes, "offers a rich, embodied visual mode of evangelism that attracts us."[3] And because the gospel offered by consumerism is driven not by moralism but by beauty (let's face it, students dress up to go to the mall, and buy what they do because of the look it gives them), Smith observes the unified message of all the stores in the mall is quite exclusive, putting to shame those who do not adore it, making it "increasingly difficult to be an infidel."[4] Smith goes on to explain the altars we find in the mall, that is, the checkout lanes where we take possession of our relics and participate in the sacrament of selfishness.

One could argue that the gospel most exported by America the past generation is the good news of a good life filled with good things. Consumer idolatry sucks the zeal out of students and refocuses their attention from the mission of God to the mission of their own happiness. I'm not saying you should boycott the mall, but I am saying you should pay attention to the idolatry it so easily fosters.

But the shopping mall is not the only temple to the idol of consumerism. Go to a theater to see a movie. Notice the surround sound and massive screen designed to wow you with the scene. Be aware that a movie involves far more than seeing or hearing only, for movie watching in a theater offers multisensory worship (smell the popcorn, feel the subwoofers, hear the music, know the effect it has on you). Entertainment has become another outlet for the consumerist god.

Even better, to observe worship in our land today, go to a large football stadium on a Saturday (or Sunday for the NFL). See those gathered, how they take great care to dress appropriately and give great homage to their object of devotion. Note the high priests in their unique garb and the devotion they cherish, a small piece of inflated leather.

The golden calf has become the oblong cowhide.

You may object, those are not really houses of worship. Or are they? The first offers the altar of consumerism and materialism. The second calls us to devotion to the god of entertainment. The third bids us bring our passion and our jerseys to give tribute to the idol of sports. By no means am I calling you a modern-day Baal worshipper if you go to a mall or a movie or enjoy sports. But neither should you be naive and think clothing, a good story line, or a sporting event hasn't become a god thing in the lives of many, including those in our churches.

 Sometimes we need to stop and ask ourselves just how much time we really need to devote to entertaining ourselves.

There are students in our churches whose devotion to Jesus is less than the devotion many have to these three places of worship. Our hearts are idol-making factories, John Calvin observed.[5] We easily take the good we have received from God and make these things gods, not unlike the heathen in Romans 1.

David Platt has exposed the consumerism of the American Dream as idolatry in his book *Radical*.[6] The American Dream for the believer is not a distraction; it is an idol. We have tried to hitch the gospel of Jesus to the American Dream, and this has failed. How many parents have I met who tell their students to get a good education, get a good job, but hardly mention walking with Jesus in the same category? We must challenge students to think differently about their affections and their possessions as they relate to the mission of God. We must help students see that receipts and calendars will reveal one's God. The American Dream has so infected our churches we can hardly see it.

## THE IDOLATRY OF THE CHRISTIAN BUBBLE

I want to look at another issue that many have seen as a distraction but I now fear has become an idol for too many. I refer to the Christian bubble, or the Christian subculture. Walk into a Christian bookstore and scan the T-shirt racks. Google "dumb church signs" or "dumb Christian T-shirts" and see what you find. Take a moment and think about all the "Christian" stuff you can see: Christian music, Christian yellow pages, Christian art, Christian fiction. Got bad breath? Buy some Testamints (they should taste like cheese). Want to get a great toy for your child? Buy a Jesus action figure.

No, please don't. Don't do that to your child, and don't do that to Jesus. You can spot something in the Christian subculture because it looks like something you would find elsewhere, costs more, and doesn't work as well!

Again, I want to be careful to say that so much we see in our Christian world today is not in itself evil or idolatrous. But the rise of the Christian subculture has confused many and has made the gospel remarkably unattractive to unbelievers (and to a lot of young believers). I have been in conversations with unchurched or dechurched friends in recent months and have seen how the Christian subculture has been more effective in turning people off to Jesus than it has been in demonstrating the aroma of Christ.

Dan Kimball's book *They Like Jesus but Not the Church* helped me see the Christian bubble as not merely an annoyance but as idolatry. At one point he identified a progression, or more accurately a declension, many believers go through to wind up in the bubble. I like what he writes and give him credit for sparking my thought on this. But what I have observed involves more than what he noted. So, with a nod to Kimball, take a look at what happens to so many of us (including me) who do love Jesus but who also grew up in the Christian subculture.

1. *We need Christ.* We all start here, dead in sin, desperately in need of Christ.

2. *We become believers.* I am talking about those who genuinely come to salvation by grace alone through faith alone because of the work accomplished by Christ alone. Christ changes our lives by His power through the cross. We have newfound joy, a hunger to grow, and begin to see our lives changing. At the same time we have a deep burden for those who do not know Jesus. We pray for them, talk to them, and hope to reach them. But something happens early in our growth in

sanctification, something we see in almost everything around us in the Christianity we see. Before long, like the frog in the kettle, we make a fundamental shift in our basic understanding of what a Christian is, away from discipleship and toward church attendance.

3. *We become a church attender.* We hear talk in our churches about faithful attendance and see it celebrated above all else. We hear less about radical obedience than Sunday school, more about attending small group than attending to our character. Before long we learn the drill: What seems to be valued more than just about anything is church attendance. We begin to see Christianity less as a movement of people daily in the culture and more as a building to attend consistently. We still care about those who do not know Christ, but we are more likely to invite them to an event than to pray for them as we had before or speak to them directly about Jesus. This shift into church-attendance-as-great-Christianity leads to the next step.

4. *We become part of the Christian subculture.* Or, the Christian bubble. Or, the Christian ghetto. Ghettoes in cities are easily recognized. They look different from other parts of the city, and most people avoid them. In our Christian bubbles we may actually confuse a good activity with the best. "We get more excited about going overseas to the mission field . . . than about the mission field we live in every day,"[7] wrote Dan Kimball. We go to "Christian" day at the theme park and put a fish on the back of our car. We start speaking Christianese, which makes us increasingly incapable of talking to people not like us. We become more like people living in a ghetto than people transformed by the gospel. Certainly, the gospel does change us, and we should look different from the world, but not in an "odd-for-God" kind of way. The change we hear championed has more to do with external conformity with other believers than demonstrating Christ to the world.

5. As a result *we become fans.* Instead of following Christ and encouraging our children to chase after Christ more than college or career, and to value self-sacrifice over self-fulfillment, we trade a

surrendered life of a follower for the more convenient life of a fan. As Kyle Idleman unpacks with great detail in *Not a Fan*, we in the bubble need a "DTR," or "define the relationship," conversation with ourselves. A fan means "an enthusiastic admirer."[8] As long as a fan is more committed than others, he is satisfied. A fan according to Idleman means Jesus is one of many, not the one and only, and you follow rules more than the Ruler. And a fan can celebrate heroic Christianity with enthusiasm, because the more enthusiastic our celebration the less we feel the need to sacrifice ourselves (or our children).

We love the story of Jim Elliot, who with his friends bravely died as a martyr in 1956 in Ecuador trying to reach a remote, unreached people group for Christ. We just don't want our children to surrender to Christ like Elliot did. We love the most popular Christian bands (I have met Christians who made an annual trip to the Dove Awards with the zeal of a Muslim going to Mecca), and even make men of God who preach the gospel into celebrities. We naturally connect to other fans who love the same music or heroes of the faith. Daily walking with Christ becomes subservient to occasional bursts of fandom.

6. *Fans then become clones.* Jesus commanded His followers to make disciples of Him, not clones of them. But an overly zealous Christian subculture easily creates the mind-set that we must look like each other to be truly spiritual. Educate your children in the approved manner, listen to the approved musicians (and by all means avoid that awful rock and roll, never taking time to be discerning regarding "Christian" music). When our daughter got her driver's license, one of the first things she did was go to the local Christian bookstore to buy books for herself. One, I told her, was a great book. One was awful, and one was borderline. In other words, just because it has the sign of the fish or "Christian" on it does not mean it does or doesn't honor Christ.

Clones often co-opt the world in a way that affirms their Christian subculture while actually mimicking the world they avoid. A student of mine observed believers who saw the Wednesday night meal at their church as functioning in the same form as a bar, just at a safe place with safe people without alcohol. This has a chilling effect on our relationship with the lost.

7. *We become awkward, especially around unbelievers.* Because our focus is the bubble, what difference does it make if those outside the bubble are impressed or influenced by me? It is too hard to convert them to my kingdom with my rules anyway. So we stay around those like us because it takes much less work to impress them. Hence, we are awkward with unbelievers, because we have no desire for their souls that compels us to care.

We go to movies and play golf or go fishing with other bubble believers, but often never even think about doing such things with the unchurched. On the rare occasion when we do find ourselves talking to the unchurched, we find ourselves uncomfortable with their language or perspective on politics or other issues. Rather than seeing conversations as an opportunity to share Christ, they make us long for fellowship with people who share our worldview. We do not find ourselves praying for others as we once did, but we do find ourselves pitying people not like us.

8. Tragically, because of some or all of the other effects of the Christian subculture, *some of us become like Jonah.* After years in the bubble, we relate to the culture around us mostly by complaining about it. "Like Jonah . . . who ran away when God told him to go to the wicked city of Ninevah (Jonah 1:3), we don't want anything to do with those who aren't following God."[9] The church becomes a place to protect us from the evil world rather than a sending base for the mission of God. We fill our calendars with activities that keep us at the safe church building, which has become more monastery than mission center. We don't think about the lostness of those who are apart from Christ, at least not as much as we think about how awful they are for being lost. As a result, we spend far more time nitpicking little disagreements over nonsense, while people are perishing all around us. I have been here too many times, and it is a sorry way to live.

Remember the Alamo? It started as a mission, became a battlefield, and is now a museum.

This is not a little issue. This is idolatry, the exchanging of the Great Commission for the Great Presumption—we presume our Christian bubble actually represents the gospel. No, that is actually what Jesus came to confront (see Matthew 23). We are not to be like the world. But our subculture is definitely not making us more like Jesus. It may make us more like the Pharisees who condemned Jesus. What happens next?

9. *We need Christ.* Not just for salvation. We are secure in Christ. But also for our sanctification. Jesus rescued us from sin in salvation, but some of us really need to be rescued as believers from the idolatry of self. We need a missional shift. We realize the gospel is for us as believers, the Great Commission is not the Great Suggestion, and that God saves us to send us into the culture to spread His love as His ambassadors.

Here is the problem: Far too many in the subculture never get here. Some walk away, becoming dechurched and often antagonistic to what they perceive as Christianity. Some become disillusioned and seek spiritual solace in other ideologies from cults to covens. But many become quite comfortable in the subculture, confusing it with authentic Christianity. We do not even see our faith being corrupted into something other than gospel-driven vitality. But for some, thankfully, through repentance and fresh spiritual eyes, we change.

10. *We become disciples.* Rescued for service by the same gospel that rescued us from sin, we see the Christian subculture as just one more idol. I have walked down this road. I am a recovering bubbleholic. And God has used friends who do not know Christ to help me see my declension. But God be praised for giving new eyes to see.

Can you identify with any of this? Being in the Christian bubble is bad; simply criticizing it may be even worse. Let's step up and lead others to burst the bubble and live like Jesus.

## THE IDOLATRY OF IMMATURITY

Another issue in student culture is the idol of immaturity. From beer commercials to sitcoms, broadcast media mockingly capitalize on, normalize, and even glamorize blatant immaturity in young men in our time. This flows out of the relatively recent development of a cultural concept of adolescence, with roots in the Industrial Revolution.[10] As I noted in *Raising the Bar*, adolescence is a reality in our time. But it is a modern reality, and while we must not ignore it, neither should we build our ministries on a concept that is quite foreign to Scripture.[11]

The wise student pastor or parent would try to understand the impact of adolescence as a part of the orthodoxy of our culture. At the same time I would argue that one of the biggest tragedies in student ministry over the last generation is the wholesale endorsement of our culture's philosophy of youth and the implications of that philosophy instead of speaking biblically and prophetically to that culture. The Bible regards young adults—like Esther, Jonathan, and Jeremiah—as capable of serving God, not stuck in a "time-out" where they have to wait.

When we see the widespread acceptance of the corollary to the theory of adolescence, the rampant celebration of immaturity in particular among young men, we should confront this, not as Puritans who simply want young men to "toe the line," but because they are missing so much in life while prolonging their childhood.

Movies with stars like Adam Sandler, Will Ferrell, Ben Stiller, and Jim Carrey (while pretty funny, I confess) have an underlying message that applauds immaturity. The problem is that off the big screen, young men in the real world emulate these movie characters but rarely make a mature decision in the end the way the guys often do in the movies.

Years ago, Terrence Moore, in an article called "Wimps and Barbarians," offered insightful commentary on young men in our day. Moore's article details the two extremes we see lived out in Western culture: Most young men tend to be either barbarians or wimps. While written some time ago, it could have just been published given the culture of immaturity promoted today.

"So prevalent are these two errant types," Moore wrote, "that the prescription for what ails our young males might be reduced to two simple injunctions: Don't be a barbarian. Don't be a wimp. What is left, *ceteris paribus*, will be a man."[12]

You will not develop a missional posture in student ministry if most of the young men are either wimps or barbarians. Moore observed how easy it is to spot a barbarian today, observing in particular their clothing, their speech, their divided lives, and the way they treat women. He noted that these young barbarians often wear a ball cap as a version of a lucky charm, finding security and courage in it like a favorite boyhood stuffed animal.

Young barbarians love sports but do not know how to act when away from the gym or ball field, so they act like they never left it. Sports can of course be a good thing, and I agree with Moore that physical training can help develop manly virtues like courage, stamina, and sportsmanship. But these immature fellows who seem so focused on the sports field and so disciplined in the weight room have a remarkable inability to apply themselves to their studies or to relationships. No wonder young men in their twenties and thirties get more excited about fantasy football than real relationships.

I think the culture at large has more barbarian young men than wimps, and the church has more wimps than barbarians. But we too have our share of barbaric young men who disrespect authority and treat young women more like property than people.

If you work with students, please help train young men to shake hands, look people in the eye, and appreciate the wisdom of those who have gone before them. Most young men I know are truly teachable but have never had anyone teach them how to relate to older men or to young women.

If you are a young man, do you find conversation with men much older than you difficult, especially on important topics?

A lot of young men in our churches relate best to young women via sarcasm and teasing (and there are a remarkably high number of young ladies who seem not to mind!). Men protect young women; they do not pester them.

One of the most vital ways you can disciple young men today is to expose them to the idolatry of immaturity and challenge these young men to be men who protect, who have conviction, who take the harder path, who see long term; challenge them to be men who long to learn, not from other barbarians, but from men of God.

But the wimp is a bigger problem in the church, a natural by-product of the combination of factory-based Christianity and the lack of missional passion to do valiant things for God. The quota for wimps has in fact been long surpassed; they are everywhere in the church. The number of single young women going to the mission field is far greater than the number of young men in my tradition. It is easier to find a hesitant young man than one focused on living fully for Christ in most churches, and that is our fault.

By wimp I do not mean a guy who is athletically challenged. Just as one can be a diminutive intellectual and be a barbarian, one can appear manly on the outside and yet be a wimp. In football we have an expression for a guy who appears manly, all muscular and athletic-looking, but stumbles off the field like a whipped two-year-old the first time he is hit. We call him the "look like Tarzan, play like Jane" guy. In short, a wimp.

Wimps are often characterized by their media. Media makes no one a wimp, but retreating to headphones or a controller instead of dealing with a challenge does. And when it comes to relationships a wimp is easily distinguished. Moore has this one pegged:

> Since he has few qualities or achievements to recommend him, he seeks to appear "interesting" or mysterious. Initially, the wimp might seem amusing to an unsuspecting young lady and very different from the insensitive jocks and rowdies she has known. Ultimately, however, the wimp seeks to draw her into his web of melancholy and self-pity. The story always ends unhappily since romance cannot be based

upon pity or the thin facade of personality. . . . The wimp will begin the relationship by saying, "You're the only one who understands me" and end it by saying, "You don't understand me at all." The truth is that there is not much to understand.[13]

If you are a guy and you have more girl friends than guy friends, you may be a wimp. I have gotten a few e-mails and other responses to that statement. But Moore notes why in the previous paragraph. You see, guy friends will confront other guys, whereas girls tend to be sympathetic. Men need men who will get up in their grill and challenge their stupidity (we, all who are male, have a remarkable propensity for stupidity), and men who are not wimps can take it, even if we do not like it. Paul challenges young Timothy to be a man of God (see 1 Timothy 6:11). We should do no less.

We need men.

## THE IDOL OF ENTITLEMENT

Cultures have orthodoxies. When in Greece I noted how community matters far more to the Greeks I met than to the typical, individualistic Americans I know. We have our orthodoxies as well, and one of the most glaring examples is entitlement. It is behind a significant part of the lobbying in Washington, DC, and it marks most who live in the West. We think we are entitled to a nice job, retirement, health care, and on and on. In reality, we are entitled to hell, judgment, and the wrath of God. Anything else we receive is grace. But believers are not immune to this entitlement mind-set.

Just yesterday I took my daughter and a friend through a fast-food drive-through. The lady in front of us had just been cut off by the person in front of her. Apparently that entitled her to give the finger to the other driver, roll down her window to curse and scream, and then unload on the poor young cashier at the window who had nothing to do with any of it. Amazing what we think we are entitled to do in this day.

But what troubles me most is the way Christians seem to feel entitled to things. Some (not most) pastors expect preferential treatment from businesses simply because they are ministers. Some church members expect preferential treatment because their family has been in a certain church for years.

I teach amazing students and spend time with wonderful young people. The overwhelming majority truly love the Lord with a thankful heart and humility. But even they can give in to entitlement. Students tend to believe they are owed a certain grade, even if using the language of "earning" it. But if a professor determines otherwise, students feel treated unfairly. A few students act as though they are entitled to get an A for showing up in class and smiling a lot. I once (only once) had a student try to go through one of my children to get me to cut them slack on an assignment. Let's just say that student never did that again after we had a nice little talk.

If you make a ball team, do not assume that entitles you to playing time.

If you go to college, do not think you are entitled to a grade you have not earned.

If you start a new job, resist the attitude that you deserve a paycheck without working hard.

Resist entitlement. Embrace gratitude.

Some time ago, our golden retriever, Precious, had to be put down. She had come to the place where she could hardly walk. She was miserable. Yet in her last few months, when Michelle and I sat on the back deck and watched the birds (we love to do that, although our children think we are hopelessly middle-aged), she always got up and came to see us, wagging her tail. If we motioned her away she simply went away. She never acted as though she were entitled to be petted because she protected our home or because she had been so loyal for so many years. No, she simply loved to be around us. No entitlement mentality.

Sometimes I really miss that dog.

The answer to entitlement is the gospel. To be reminded that God owes us nothing but hell and we can do nothing to earn His favor, that He alone is the grace-giver—that reality fosters humble gratitude over prideful entitlement.

I am confident I have missed some of the idolatrous tendencies in your church or region. But you can see them everywhere, just as Paul saw the city of Athens filled with idolatry in Acts 17. Be aware of them and confront them with the gospel. Let the Holy Spirit and the Sword of the Spirit, the Word of God, constantly search for areas to be surgically removed through the faithful preaching of the Word.

## REVIEW AND APPLICATION

- What idols entice your students?
- Gather a group of mature students and leaders and discuss the idols in your area, including both the obviously evil attractions (pornography, for instance) and those good things that may have become a god thing (relationships, Christian subculture, material things).
- How can you teach the gospel in such a way that you confront these idols? What steps can you take to destroy them?
- In 2 Chronicles 34 we read about a young man named Josiah. At age sixteen he openly followed God, and at age twenty when he was given full power as king, he immediately set out to destroy the idols in his nation. Should we have the same zeal to confront the idols that keep us from the mission to which God has called us?

# CHAPTER 7

# MISSIONAL FAMILIES

### *Chicago and New York*

Chicago and New York tower above most cities as among the greatest in America and in the world.

When our son Josh turned twelve, I took him to Chicago for a dad-son rite-of-passage getaway. We ministered with the Armitage Baptist Church in the inner city, saw a Cubs game at Wrigley Field, the Michael Jordan movie at the IMAX theater, and had some memorable conversations. When Hannah turned sixteen, I took her on a similar trip to Manhattan where we stayed in Times Square. We spent some time with a young church plant called the Gallery Church and enjoyed shopping, fine dining, and a carriage ride around Central Park. As with Josh, we also shared some very important conversations.

## FAMILIES MATTER

The first institution given to us by God was the home. The first time God said it was *very good* in Scripture was when He made Adam and Eve. Student ministry over the past generation has, whether intentionally or not, pushed the family to the side. But the family should be at the heart of any student ministry. Student pastors and ministries to students should partner with Christian homes in the gospel work of raising a missional generation. These families should also serve as role models for the many young people who come from difficult or even destructive homes. The family centered on Christ offers a beautiful picture of the gospel.

The family is the primary learning community for children. It offers all the best forms of education, from lecturing (parents seem gifted at that, don't they?), to life-on-life mentoring, to role-playing, and others. This is why what we say as parents must be demonstrated with consistency in our lives. Some today perceive student ministry as an adversary of the family or vice versa, working against one another. I would argue that the strongest student ministries recognize the vital role of both the local church family and the nuclear family. When the nuclear family fails, the local church family has a greater responsibility to demonstrate biblical relationships to those affected students.

Let's face it: Being a parent has to be the most encouraging and discouraging, challenging and fulfilling, joyful and sorrowful, exhilarating and gut-wrenching thing you can ever do. Michelle and I thank God that our children love Jesus and His gospel, not that they are perfect (they have us for parents!). We have seen the faithfulness of God. But we have also seen a tendency for some Christian parents to focus on avoiding evil to the neglect of a positive focus on the gospel. I would argue biblically that nothing a parent does for his child matters more than helping that child stake out a missional lifestyle centered on the gospel regardless of her vocation or location.

In his book *The Age of Opportunity*, Paul Tripp observes professionally what I have seen anecdotally for years: Most Christian parents are afraid of their children when they become teens. He believes the cynicism toward teens should be challenged and discarded. "Although they would never say it," Tripp writes, "the working theology that hides behind this view is that the truths of Scripture, the power of the Gospel, biblical communication, and godly relationship are no match for the teen years."[1] Tripp argues eloquently what we as parents discovered, that the teen years are the best years of parenting, what he calls the Age of Opportunity. These years of struggle, of growth and change, of maturation, will challenge students and their parents at every level of their walk with God. But do we see these as the greatest years or the most fearful?

The Rosenthal Effect, or Pygmalion Effect, shows that the expectations we put on those we teach have a remarkable impact on their performance. In Acts 11:23 we read how Barnabas "came and saw the grace of God" when he arrived to lead the new believers at Antioch. As a result, he rejoiced. Why did Barnabas rejoice? He saw the grace of God. Why did he see the grace of God? He was *looking* for it.

▶ Parents must look for the ways God is working in their children. He is working! Discipline them we must, but we must encourage them as well.

One of the most exciting days of a parent is when their little one takes her first step. That first step, wobbly and imperfect as it is, brings screams of joy from the parent and bewilderment from the child, who is not quite aware of what she did. But the same parent who gives such effusive praise can in later years focus excessively on hammering a teenager for her failures while missing opportunities to give unashamed encouragement and hope.

Do you believe God has a plan for your child's life? I'm sure you do. Do you truly believe your primary role in the life of that bundle of eternity entrusted to you is to help that child live for the glory and the Story of God? If so, that will be at the heart of your parenting and will involve far more than just getting her to the youth group. This means we have to do far more than what most parents consider as top importance: getting their children to act right. No, we need to help children believe right and experience the reality of the gospel. The result will be right behavior, but as mentioned previously, focusing on behavior alone can lead to legalism.

Millennials today want relationships that last. Almost every time I mention to a student group that my wife and I have been married thirty years, they break out in clapping and cheers. They do not see enough marriages that last. But compared to my parents' generation (my parents just celebrated their sixtieth wedding anniversary), Millennials do not embrace marriage as quickly as in the past. They are marrying much later, if at all. For instance, 44 percent of eighteen- to twenty-five-year-old boomers (my generation) were married in 1970, compared to 15 percent of Millennials today. The average age of a female's first marriage has increased from 20.8 in 1970 to 25.5 now, and in the same time the age of men has gone up from 23.2 to 27.5. Perhaps most significant is the rise in young adults who cohabit, from around 10 percent in the 1960s to about two-thirds of young adults today. That is remarkable but not encouraging.[2]

Stop for just a moment if you are a dad or mom or hope to be one. Think about this: Dads, only you can be the dad to your children. Your student pastor cannot; neither can your pastor. The same is true for you, moms. Outside of your personal relationship to Christ there is nothing more important on this earth, should God grant you these relationships, than being a godly spouse, and then a godly parent. Do not professionalize the family by expecting a children's pastor or student pastor to do what God has ordained for you to do.

If you are a student pastor remember this: Short of disqualifying yourself for ministry, one of the worst things you can do is to sacrifice your family on the altar of ministry to other families. Value your family. Value the families of your students. Make sure the home is a healthy, gospel-centered environment. The great Reformer Martin Luther understood this. Before the Reformation began he wrote, "If ever the church is to flourish again, one must begin by instructing the young."[3]

The truth is, the coming generation of students in our churches must become missional if we are to thrive again as a Christian movement in the West. I have no delusions that my generation will ever fully grasp this, but helping parents understand their role in the missional formation of our children matters, which is why I wrote this book with parents in mind. The programs of organized church simply cannot teach and model everything students need to walk with Christ for a lifetime. God has ordained that role first to the family, as well as to the church. Faith involves living a lifestyle, not just mastering content.

> "The solution isn't to kick the traditional student ministry up a notch. The solution is to reexamine how the Bible should guide our framework to develop students and encourage the parents and adults who influence them." — Steve Wright[4]

Parents have a remarkably influential role in whether students actually get the things that matter. "The best way to get most youth more involved in and serious about their faith communities," Kenda Creasy Dean writes, "is to get their parents more involved in and serious about their faith communities."[5]

Whether we want to admit it or not, our children for the most part will become like us. Most parents of teens tend to make controlling the behavior of their children the primary focus in their spiritual development. This is important. Hormonal changes, the growing awareness of choices, and the increasing freedom of students can lead students to make wrong choices and behave badly on a frequent basis. I agree with Tripp, however, that the most effective way to help students behave is to focus less on behavior and more on Christ and His mission.

A parent may have to act like a policeman at times, but the primary role of a parent is to teach by precept and example, not to uphold the rules. Tripp argues that our role is to equip students for the war that is the Christian life in a fallen world, and this starts by "asking what is really important to us."[6] And the Bible gives us clear instruction about what should matter most to us.

## BIBLICAL WISDOM FOR FAMILIES

Deuteronomy 6 contains priceless information for parents and families. Verses 4-5 are commonly known as the Shema, which is the first Hebrew word of the text, meaning "hear." Jesus quoted the Shema in the Great Commandment (see Matthew 22:35-40). Some have called it the John 3:16 of the Old Testament. Read verses 4-9 and see the great vision given to parents:

> Hear, O Israel: The LORD our God, the LORD is one. You shall love the LORD your God with all your heart and with all your soul and with all your might. And these words that I command you today shall be on your heart. You shall teach them diligently to your children, and shall talk of them when you sit in your house, and when you walk by the way, and when you lie down, and when you rise. You shall bind them as a sign on your hand, and they shall be as frontlets between your eyes. You shall write them on the doorposts of your house and on your gates.

Several years ago, I spoke at a prayer conference. I focused at one point on treating youth as young men and women capable of significant spiritual challenges, including praying God-sized prayers. A lady came to speak to me afterward. This woman obviously saw herself as quite spiritual. She proceeded to throw her student pastor under the bus, complaining about his failure to help her fifteen-year-old son grow spiritually. I proceeded to turn to Deuteronomy 6:4-9. I showed her how she and her husband, not a student pastor in particular or the church in general, had primary responsibility for the spiritual growth of her son. The church would certainly play a role, but she and her husband should focus on teaching her son the things of God and tell the student pastor he could focus more on reaching students who were not believers instead. That was not the answer she wanted! But I am sure it was what she needed.

I confess to the simple belief that the answer to problems in the home is the gospel. And the way to prevent many problems and, more importantly, prepare your children for a life of walking with Christ is to make a passionate commitment to growing a gospel-centered home, a home in which every decision is based on the glory of God and furthering the gospel.

If you are a parent, how will you leave a legacy for your children that will lead them and the generations following to love God? Look at Deuteronomy 6. What should be demonstrated in the home above all else? Morality? Achievement? Possessions? This passage unambiguously declares that a love for God with all our heart, soul, and strength matters above all else.

The Great Commandment should be central in any Christian home. In fact, if your home demonstrates a devotion to the Great Commandment and the Great Commission you can lead your children to missional lives. This means more than memorizing and reciting these two commands; it means learning how the whole of Scripture relates to them as well. In your decisions as a family, do you seek first to listen to God? Does your family put following God and His Word above all else? If so, does a passion for the lost and love for neighbors, literal and figurative, have a central place in your home? Do we sometimes miss the centrality of loving God above all when we tell our children to get a good education and good job, but fail to place as much emphasis on hearing and loving God? Do we affirm in our teaching and our living that there is only one God, and only one way to have a right relationship with that God?

As our children entered high school and middle school, respectively, we bought our current home with this in mind. We sought a home that (1) was in a neighborhood of folks not actively churched (and we have the greatest neighbors ever!) and (2) was designed to help focus on being together—a large great room with TV and computer all in one large space. Our children spent little time in their last years at home in their rooms because we had taken practical steps, even in our floor plan, to create an environment of togetherness. We intentionally did not allow a TV or computer in our children's rooms so that we would have more time to interact, talking about and modeling the things we read in these verses.

The primary responsibility for educating children to be godly and live missionally falls to parents. Deutoronomy 6 says these truths must be in your heart, Dad, and yours too, Mom. No, you will never live them out perfectly, but our children should see our trajectory set in that direction. The phrase "teach them diligently" literally means to "sharpen the knife." We should be sharpening our children (and the church should be involved in this as well) to be ready for life as missionaries when they leave home. This will be much easier if the home in which they grow up functions as a missionary station. For some homes this is a radical shift. But the best way to protect your children from evil is to help them give their lives to what is good, and nothing is better than the good news in Christ.

We have developed an institutional mind-set in the church that has compartmentalized our lives. Scripture does not support the notion that spiritual training is primarily the job of the church, and in particular with teens the task of a specialized student pastor. When parents do not teach their children diligently but instead give them morality or anything short of a robust, gospel-focused life, they enter the world dull, not sharp. Because they cannot easily discern good from evil, they make bad friends and bad choices when they begin living on their own. We must help them with life skills and wisdom as well as with knowledge.

How does this look practically? The good news is that Deuteronomy 6:6-9 spells out the "how" very well. It certainly involves active participation in a gospel-centered local church, and it includes imparting a vision for the salvation of both neighbors and nations. I like to think about these verses this way:

**These words that I command you today shall be on your heart.** Children should see their parents spending time in God's Word, daily demonstrating Christlike character and being concerned for the unbelieving world. This includes family worship, family discussions, and family participation in the local church.

**Teach them diligently to your children.** We should be instructing children, particularly when young, about the things of God. This means showing how all of life, not just our "spiritual" or "church" life, relates to Jesus. The idea that explicitly "spiritual" things are good and all material things are bad was an early heresy called gnosticism, and an overreaching Christian subculture, as noted earlier, gives a practical example of adopting that mind-set today. We are to help children see how to live out a biblical worldview.

Certainly we protect them and their innocence when young, but as they mature through the teen years they grow in making decisions in all arenas of life from a biblical perspective. As a result, they own their faith by the time they leave the constant influence of their parents' faith. Instead of raising them to be faithful citizens in a religious subculture, we help them see all of creation through biblical eyes.

**Talk of them when you sit in your house.** Family mealtime provides one of the greatest places for teaching everything from civility to life lessons. This was a very big deal in our home. Research has shown the significant impact of regular family meals. If we do not talk about Jesus to others, perhaps it is because we do not talk about Him much in our homes.

**When you walk by the way.** The church and the home are not the only places to learn how to live and share Christ. Our activities, from talking to the waitress at the restaurant (and tipping well!) to being courteous at the mall, help to show how to live out our faith rather than confining it to our house and the church house. In addition, talking to neighbors about things that matter helps children see the world through missionary eyes.

**When you lie down, and when you rise.** Bedtime, especially for younger children, provides a great time for prayer and instruction in spiritual things. Sit at the end of the bed a little longer and remind them of God's love, provision, and work each day. Praying together is important. The staggering majority of Christian families do not pray together regularly. We can hardly complain about prayer being taken from the public schools if we are not praying in our Christian homes.

**Bind them as a sign on your hand, and they shall be as frontlets between your eyes. You shall write them on the doorposts of your house and on your gates.** I suppose this could include Christian symbols and expressions, but it is vital to saturate every fiber of our being, the very fabric of our lives, with the gospel. Our interaction with neighbors should bring glory to God and communicate Christ to those who need Him. We need to do a lot more than buy our children "Christian" T-shirts.

These simple words from Deuteronomy call for a lot of parents in our churches to refocus dramatically. Help parents move in this direction. Encourage them. Take a moment and think: What is the place of the Great Commandment and the Great Commission in your home, not only in your rhetoric but also in the way you live your life before your children? The greatest missionary force in America today sleeps in our bedrooms. Let us equip them and engage them now.

## MISSIONAL PARENTING

Zac Sunderland demonstrates the impact of parents on a young man who would not settle for hanging out and playing games all day. This young man sailed a boat around the world by himself at age seventeen. He started at age sixteen, essentially homeschooled himself, fought off pirates near Indonesia, and became the youngest person to sail solo around the world.[7] Why would a young man do this? Because he could. And because his parents believed in him. Zac grew up in a sailing family. Oh, and he also is a believer whose family encouraged him from a biblical perspective. Not every child needs to do something so dramatic, but every child has been created uniquely by God and can make a remarkable impact for Jesus.

Too many well-intentioned parents demonstrate more caution than encouragement for their children to live radically committed to Jesus. In 1992 the Earth Summit issued the Rio Declaration. The declaration articulated a posture of taking precautions against activities potentially harmful to the environment. This view, known as the precautionary principle, has since become increasingly prohibitive, creating the idea that "even if you can't prove scientifically that harm is happening, this uncertainty should not prevent you from stopping the suspected harm."[8] This attitude has since shaped much of environmental policy in the U.S. and globally. I believe as stewards of God's creation we have a responsibility not to trash the earth, but this position has allowed for rather extreme views of conservation to be considered mainstream.

I fear a parental version of the precautionary principle hinders many students from flourishing in their walk with Christ. We fear our children will not be liked, so we focus on a school environment that protects them above one that prepares them for a life focused on the mission of God. We force our children to play Amateur Athletic Union (AAU) ball or join intensive leagues when they do not even like the sport that much, but we are sure their participation will better their life experience. I have personally seen families sacrifice corporate worship on Sundays for a ball team and then wonder why their children had no interest in church later. I could give many other examples, and by no means am I saying all parents do this. But research is clear that parents of Millennials overprotect their children (have you heard the term "helicopter parent"?[9]), and this well-intentioned but often misplaced parental focus can hinder children from growing into the passionately missional believers God made them to be and they often want to be themselves.

I am not saying to remove all boundaries. We must protect our children. But if at age eighteen they have no ability to operate in a grown-up world, we have overprotected, not sharpened. Dr. James Dobson of Focus on the Family told a story years ago of children at play.

When released for playtime, they spread out across the large playground, running along the perimeter fence, enjoying themselves as children do. Then the fence was removed. When playtime came, they huddled anxiously in the middle of the playground. Once the fence was restored, they returned to their jubilant play.[10] The gospel and its truth should be the fence we teach our children. Not the law and ritual and legalistic rules, but truth flowing out of a love for God and a concern for others.

## PRACTICAL MISSIONAL IDEAS

Often when I speak, I ask those in attendance to raise their hands if they were raised in a Christian home. In most cases, about 80 to 90 percent raise their hands. I then ask all those who raised hands if they remember ever talking about reaching their neighbors. I clarify that I'm asking not only if their families were consistently seeking to share the gospel or doing anything to reach neighbors but whether they even talked about it at home. Around 10 to 20 percent respond yes. Too many of us raise our children as if we were atheists in our neighborhoods. This is the direct result of institutional Christianity built on a factory model that expects little beyond church attendance and a basic level of morality. We can do more for our neighbors and more for our children.

- Do something regularly for and with neighbors. Start with being a good neighbor. We have done block parties and hosted Pampered Chef parties, among other activities.
- Use your talents and gifts where you are. Missional means living out and sharing the gospel in the context of who you are and where you live. For example, Michelle is great at making crafts. Every year she makes each neighbor family a Christmas craft. One neighbor recently said the greatest Christmas gift she ever received was the first craft Michelle made. Our children played ball with the neighbor children, took care of pets, and did other normal things normal neighbors do. Hint: If you are bound up

in the Christian subculture, you will only do these things with and for your "Christian friends" and your children will likely never be missional.

- Plan activities in the community, with your local church, and so on. My colleague George Robinson took his whole family on a mission trip to Nepal.
- Show missional living as you go. At restaurants, we always pray for our servers and leave a good tip. We have seen servers come to Christ. If the only time we talk about Jesus is with Christian friends or at the church building, we do not exhibit a missional mind-set.

Missional means much more than a verbal witness, but it doesn't mean less than that. Alisa and Kevin and their two children offer a beautiful picture of a missional family. Here is part of their story:

**Alisa (mom):** I surrendered my life to full-time missions at age twelve. I went on staff with Cru (the U.S. ministry of Campus Crusade for Christ International) right out of college and two years later met Kevin (dad). Kevin and I served with the adult ministry of Cru for eighteen years and saw many people come to know Jesus. Kevin has had the privilege of sharing Christ in Russia, Prague, Croatia, Africa, and Argentina and Bulgaria.

As a parent with older children I see now how so many of the things we were involved in has impacted their lives to share Jesus also. We made a decision along the way that we wanted our lives to reflect the belief in Jesus that we professed. If our children didn't see us trust Jesus in day-to-day life, how would they ever be able to trust Him?

God gave us three children. Allison came to know Jesus at age six. A few years later she led her brother, Mark, to know Jesus. A few years after that, Mark led Luke to know Jesus. In 2005, we took our whole family to Prague for a month to do outreach there with adult ministry of Campus Crusade.

The next year, Allison went to East Asia for five weeks. When she told me that she wanted to go, I was hesitant, as I didn't know the people personally that she was going with and five weeks without us seemed like a long time for a sixteen-year-old. The first week that she was there, I didn't even know what city she was in. It was awesome, though, after a few weeks into the trip when she called to tell me in code language that she was able to share Christ with five of her middle school girls and three of them gave their lives to Him.

Four years ago, when Kevin and I felt the call of God to start Student Venture in Raleigh, a Cru ministry to middle school and high school students, we knew that our children would be part of that as they have been in everything else we have done in our life.

**Allison (daughter):** I have been a leader in Student Venture all through college. While in college, I helped begin Student Venture in two schools, St. David's and Broughton High School. This has been the greatest joy for me while in my years of college. In October 2010, we planned an outreach with the Broughton volleyball teams. I was given the opportunity to talk to the team after practice that would lead to inviting them to come the next day for pizza and to hear a NCSU volleyball player share her testimony at the house of one of the girls on the team. At the end of our time together there, I asked all the girls to give me their contact info if they would like to be in a Bible study, and all of them indicated yes! The Bible study continued the rest of that year till they graduated. Four of the girls came to Christ. When they came back to school, all five of the girls were passionate about telling their friends about Jesus.

**Mark (son):** By the time I reached the sixth grade, I had become an avid golfer like my dad. I started thinking about how cool would it be if I were to organize a golf clinic where Bobby Clampett (a professional golfer and a family friend) would come instruct my sixth grade friends and then share his testimony. I had seen my dad do this sort of thing through his ministry a year before with Mr. Clampett.

When I was in the seventh grade, I attended Cru summer staff conference with my parents. That whole summer I felt like God was saying to me, "Mark, it is your turn now to give your assets and talents back to Me." I knew that God had given me the game of golf and that He intended it for more than just my pleasure. As a middle schooler, I was convinced that my mission field was the golf course.

I developed an outreach with the help of pro golfer Webb Simpson. Starting with the idea of a day tournament, it morphed into a weekend retreat at Pinehurst. We made the plans, and the first year we had sixty-six high school guys and nothing but praise from the golfers and their parents. Even to this day I receive notes and e-mails from parents and students alike who are so thankful for the way the weekend impacted their lives or their son's life. There were also e-mails from kids telling us that because of the influence of the tournaments they now wanted to go to church for the first time and that they finally understood the gospel.

In every church, we have families who can be an example to their children and the rest of the church body of the way God can use them for His glory.

## A WORD TO MINISTERS ABOUT RAISING CHILDREN

This book is not only for student pastors, but because many who read this will be in student ministry, I want to talk to you about an issue I see far too often in your world. Earlier in the chapter, I mentioned this briefly, but it warrants specific attention. I refer to the tendency of well-meaning student pastors to sacrifice their own families while ministering to the families of others.

Ministry is about pressure—not avoiding it or surviving it but rather thriving in the midst of ministry pressures. It is about seeing the glory and Story of God lived out in our lives as we fulfill our calling. Paul gives helpful instructions regarding pastors in 1 Timothy 3, specifically addressing the home in verses 4-5.

That leads me to the question I hear often from young ministers, student pastors, and seminarians: How do you thrive in ministry while not destroying your family?

First, **be a growing, passionate, genuine Christ follower**. Do not roll your eyes and think, "Well, of course." The destruction that comes to a minister's home comes from neglecting this more than any other factor. Admit you are at your best a sinner in need of daily grace. Preach the gospel to yourself daily. Be marked by prayer and devotion to the Word. Be accountable to others. You will not be perfect, but you must be consistent. You will fail your spouse. You will fail your children. They will fail you. Do not create added pressure from an inconsistent devotional life or a life lacking in integrity.

If you "walk with Jesus" simply because you are on staff at a church, your children will know. The inconsistency of a parent in ministry has a devastating impact on children. If Jesus is not more vital to you than anything else, He will become unimportant to them.

Next, **be spouse and parent first, minister and leader second**. I remember early in ministry hearing priorities like this: God first, then ministry, and if you take care of your ministry, God will take care of your family. That approach has failed in many a minister's home. You don't have to sacrifice your family on the altar of ministry. Student pastor, you do not have to put the children of others ahead of your own. In fact, you must not.

I think of a student pastor I will call Jack. As a classic people pleaser, he was a good fit for the youth ministry culture of today. But his wife got seconds, and then so did his children. So she left. I recall John the workaholic. John did not finish his football career or his education, so he felt he constantly had to prove his worth. He neglected his family in pursuit of approval. He is no longer in ministry.

Third, **do not make your family an idol**. Don't be like a man I will call Bill who grew up in a tough home. He wanted to be a good husband and dad. But he was lazy. He obsessed over his family and ignored others he was called to serve. He used his family as an excuse for not working. And he got fired. He eventually got things together but admits he wasted a big opportunity by overcompensating for his unhappy childhood.

We must help our children know that family is more important than other relationships in our lives, but even they are not as important as Jesus. The glory of God and the worship of King Jesus, and the sacrifices that come with our submission to Him, must be seen as valuable to our children. I was gone a lot in our children's lives, yet they love ministry. My wife is the main reason. Throughout their childhood, she demonstrated both a deep love for Christ and a strong commitment to God's call on our family, which included my being gone a lot.

Once when Hannah was young, I was lying on her bed before leaving on a trip. She said, "Daddy, I am gonna glue you to the bed." I told her how much I loved her and how I would rather be home always, but Jesus was going to let me help some others for a couple of days. And, I explained to her that if I did not consistently obey Jesus, one day that would be more harmful than helpful for her. I wasn't sure if she understood then, but she does now.

Fourth, **know the pressure points of your family**. Your family is not exactly like mine. You must know your family's needs and their strengths and weaknesses. For me, travel has been an area that causes pressure; Michelle and I have sought to make it a positive. For you, it may be long hours at a church building night after night. Be aware of the places to be most on guard. For instance:

- You and your spouse must be devoted to the message and the mission of God. A workaholic husband is no worse than a stubborn wife. I am so grateful that Michelle loves God deeply and believes in the ministry to which God has called us both.
- You must be aware of the intersection of life stages and the

pressure points of ministry. When Josh hit sixth grade he needed me more. I traveled far less that year. During Hannah's senior year I took a break from writing books and traveling so much. There are seasons our children need us more.

- Compensate for the more hectic seasons. Plan a weeklong vacation after the busiest season. Build in an extra day off. Be there for the field trip. In all my traveling I never missed the births of our children or their birthdays. Be there for special occasions. I missed almost none of our kids' ball games (and I was usually the loudest dad in the stands!).
- When a difficult time comes, drop other stuff.

Fifth, **cultivate your family relationships**.

- Every day do something in their world.
- Seek to make the two best places on earth your home and your church.
- Find what your kids do and do it with them. This is huge.
- Note that sometimes a person, usually a coward, will try to hurt you through your children or try to hurt your children, and some will succeed. Help your children see that Jesus is as real in times of pain as He is in times of joy.
- Do special things with them. Josh and I have been to a lot of ball games, and when Hannah turned sixteen, I took her to Times Square.

Sixth, **lead your family spiritually**. Family worship, gospel outreach, family conversations, rites of passage, and your own example contribute to this.

Finally, **get your children involved in ministry they love and thrive in**. Help them, especially by their high school years, to own a ministry. Josh began traveling with me to play drums as a fourteen-year-old. He still does, and I love it. He has become a great drummer, but more than that he's become a great young man of God. He also loves cities and has been on mission trips to several great cities. Hannah has mentored middle schoolers, and in her senior year began singing with our church's praise team (with her brother, which is cool for their dad and mom). She has also been on mission trips to four continents.

God has been very good to me in ministry, often in spite of me. But nothing I will do matters as much as seeing our children walk with God. That does not just happen; we must be strategic as parents to see ministry become a wonderful place to raise children.

## REVIEW AND APPLICATION

- How many students do you know who come from strong Christian homes? How can you help those homes grow in a missional focus? How can you help believing parents in single or blended homes?
- Many students come from difficult homes or homes in which parents are not believers. How can you invest in these students, and involve families in your church to invest, to help them grow in their faith?
- Read again Deuteronomy 6:4-9. In what area(s) can you involve families more in student ministry?

# CHAPTER 8

# MISSIONAL VISION

### Chiang Mai, Thailand

Chiang Mai is an urban jungle of traffic, markets, congestion, and community set in the middle of the tropical jungle of Southeast Asia. Thailand's beauty has made it a tourist destination globally, but there is a dark side. By some estimates, Thailand also has the distinction of leading the world in the sexual exploitation of women.

Our daughter Hannah joined a group of students and me on her first trip out of the country. Hannah, like so many young people I have known, simply needed to get out of the country doing mission work to give her a global vision for the Great Commission. It could have been somewhere else, but for her it happened to be Thailand. Always an adventurer, Hannah fit right in with the team as we made the trek half-way around the world. Since then she has been to a total of four continents on mission and several major U.S. cities.

## A GLOBAL VISION

Nothing can help a student grasp a missional vision like getting out of the country and engaging in hands-on ministry globally. How many of your students have been out of the country on a mission trip? How many will go this year? Perhaps the most positive shift in student ministry over the past two decades has been the dramatic trend of taking students to the nations.

Getting students out of the country on mission should be a top priority of student ministries. Mormons, who do not have the gospel, raise money all through their childhood to go on a two-year mission they fund themselves. Could we not expect our students who have Jesus to take at least one trip overseas in their time in student ministry? And if not by then, before they finish college? Some do more, serving for a year overseas in a "gap year" following high school. I know as parents one of the best things we did for our children was to help them see God at work globally. In addition to Hannah's international experiences, our son Josh has been all over Europe, from London to Paris to Rome. That was his senior trip with a Christian school, and while not technically a mission trip it nevertheless showed him much about this big world. He has been on mission trips to Latin America and to major cities in the U.S. He has a particular love for the cities of our land.

My friends Jeff Lovingood and Brian Mills have a specific strategy for involving students in mission trips with Long Hollow Baptist Church near Nashville, Tennessee. Middle school students have regional experiences, high school students begin having national opportunities, and older high school and college students can travel internationally. Jeff Borton, coauthor of *Simple Student Ministry*, has woven missions into the fabric of the student ministry at Christ Fellowship in Miami. They take teams out of the country, but also invest in the international mission field at their doorstep. While every church has different opportunities, resources, and challenges, a missional church has a heart for the whole world, starting with local neighborhoods and stretching to the ends of the earth. It must be both-and, not either-or.

In this chapter I want to push you to think about involving students in mission trips as part of a larger missional strategy. I would suggest a fourfold strategy, but you must constantly—through word, example, and structure—remind students all these fit into the larger mission of the ministry and are not compartmentalized trips. First, take some trips to the nations. Second, go to a major U.S. city. Third, set aside a week or more to be on mission in your own community. Finally, intentionally step into the new missions frontier provided by social media. I will not spend much time here on the third aspect of this approach, because chapter 9 will deal in more detail with sharing Christ in your own community. I would simply say that none of these four steps will do more to create a missional culture without a healthy emphasis on the local step as foundational to the rest.

 If at all possible, see to it that students in your church get out of the country on a mission trip before they finish high school.

If you take twenty people overseas on a trip, there is a good chance one or two will end up on the mission field. If you take a significant number of students on mission trips *and* help them see that they can live the same at home as they do overseas, these trips can help engender a missional mind-set. This is multiplied as you encourage more and more parents to come along. Having as many parents as students on an overseas mission trip is not a bad thing. Mission trips can in fact be a laboratory to test the ability of those who go to live like a missionary.

## REACH THE NATIONS

Go to nations. If God stops you, go to a city.

This has become a mantra of mine as I teach at Southeastern Seminary. Instead of saying, "God, if You call me I will go anyplace," just plan to go unless He stops you. That is a different perspective. Go with a green light until He gives you a red light.

One of the best ways to learn to be a missionary is to take a mission trip. Yes, this can contribute to event-driven ministry if we approach it as separate from everything else we do. But on a variety of levels, there is something very positive about immersing yourself in another culture for a week or two.

If you issue a challenge to get students out of the country, you have to help students who want to do this (and believe me, many will) to get there. This includes budgeting and raising support. But some will ask you, why go to the nations? When you read the Great Commission passages in the Gospel records and Acts you see a straightforward, clear mission. Read them, or better, memorize them (italics are added here for emphasis):

- Matthew 28:19: "Go therefore and make disciples of *all nations*."
- Mark 16:15: "Go into *all the world* and proclaim the gospel to the whole creation."
- Luke 24:47: "That repentance and forgiveness of sins should be proclaimed in his name *to all nations*."
- John 20:21: "As the Father has sent me, even so I am sending you." (*Implied: to the whole world as Jesus came to the whole world;* see also John 3:16-17.)
- Acts 1:8: "You will be my witnesses in Jerusalem and in all Judea and Samaria, and *to the end of the earth*."

While each passage offers its own unique focus, what is clear in all of them is this: We have a mission to take the message to the whole world. I recently stood with a team of my students at the Cape of Good Hope, the southernmost spot in Africa. We literally stood at the ends of the earth in that great continent. We need to take all the energy students have for winning video games or shopping for fashionable bargains and redirect that into accomplishing the mission of God.

If you stood before a group of believers and asked them to raise their hands if they were called by God to tell others about Christ, all having read these verses would raise their hands. But if you asked them whether they were called to take this message to the nations, you will likely get a different response. I have asked this many times. We are all called in some way to advance the gospel, making disciples among the nations as we go. The verses on the previous page and the tenor of all Scripture make this more than clear.

We seem to think that the only people called to reach the nations are those who are going as international career missionaries, appointed by a mission board, a church, or a ministry. The mission of God that compelled Christ to come into the world now compels us to go to the nations. Yes, we can help do that by praying. Yes, we can help by giving. But we can also go, many of us. We can:

- Help businessmen who love Jesus and travel abroad see themselves as missionaries and equip them in that role.
- Challenge young people to get out of the country before finishing high school.
- Give young adults a vision to spend some or all of their lives overseas.
- Challenge retired believers to take trips to the nations.
- Set aside a part of our time and resources to go ourselves.
- Seriously consider whether we should spend our lives elsewhere for the gospel.
- Ask ourselves what talent, gift, and/or passion has God given us that we can use to reach the nations.
- For those who live in the U.S., "go" by reaching those who have come from all over the globe to us.

If God so loved the world that He sent His Son for us, would we not likewise care for the nations if we truly follow Him? "I am convinced," David Platt writes in *Radical Together*, "that Satan, in a sense, is just fine with missional churches in the West spending the overwhelming majority of our time, energy, and money on trying to reach people right around us."[1] As I read his book the thing that hit me most was how many in his church committed 2 percent of their year for specific missions focus. I prayerfully committed to spend 10 percent of the rest of my life going outside the United States and doing what I am most passionate about: equipping leaders and reaching people through church planting. So this year I will spend two weeks in Kiev teaching at the Kiev Theological Seminary and helping church plants. I will spend another week teaching at the Canadian Southern Baptist Seminary. That is my giftedness and my passion. I hope to do this until my last breath.

What is your plan to reach the nations? How are you using your influence to encourage others in this focus? Is your vision as big as the planet? Sadly, I have too many seminary students who feel a call to go to the nations whose Christian parents are not happy about that fact. We who lead churches must do a better job of teaching a gospel-driven, global Christianity.

When I finished seminary, I had a keen awareness of the need for a church to reach its community with the gospel. I also had a conviction about the nations, which basically consisted of having some focus annually on missions abroad. But now I think our local church vision should be global from the start. We need a vision as big as the heart of God, and a desire to build the kingdom more than our own little empires. Fortunately, many pastors and leaders get that. I still run into the occasional believer who questions why we focus on the nations. But those are rare, and increasingly more common are those who have a vision like that in the Gospels.

As you reflect on the coming year, what can you and your students do to reach the nations?

## THINGS TO CONSIDER AS YOU GO TO THE NATIONS

I do not have the space to develop a whole plan for going overseas, but let me give a few general points of advice:

**When you go, go on a *mission* trip, not just a trip.** Do not take students on a glorified sightseeing and shopping tour. Make sure sharing the gospel is integral to the journey. Yes, build homes, host sports camps, and help the needy, but do not teach students by your practice that the gospel is unimportant as long as we just show up.

**Go with your denominational missions group, a well-regarded parachurch ministry, or someone you know and trust.** Sadly, there are plenty of opportunists out there with more zeal than wisdom. If you are going to invest time and money in a mission trip, make sure it is effective (that means your primary goal is not to give your students a good trip, but to help those on the field).

**Invest in a sustainable ministry if possible.** Recently the notion of being "sustainable" has developed a connection with ecology. But what about theology? In this case I am not thinking of the biblical and theological implications of the gospel on the environment, although I am grateful we are becoming better at such conversations. I wonder whether or not those of us who follow Christ, and especially those of us who serve as leaders of the church, give enough attention to sustainable ministry, or to use a more biblical expression, "fruit that remains." Does our practice of theology demonstrate a short-term, event-driven ideology, or does our understanding of the gospel help us focus on long-term effectiveness? If we're not careful, we can think more about the thrill of being "on mission" in another place than about the sustainability of the work we do on such trips.

Our church has for years worked with a ministry led by a Southeastern graduate from India in his native land, digging wells, sharing Christ, planting churches, and training pastors. We have partnered with similar ministries in Greece and other places. Sustainability helps make mission trips a lasting part of the missional lives of students.

Consider all the trips you have taken for the kingdom of God. Think about the exact places and faces. Today, what continues to make an impact for the Lord because of your time? For example, I am grateful to have participated in the training of hundreds of pastors at an evangelism conference in Ukraine. Why? Because Pastor Johnny Hunt of First Baptist Church in Woodstock, Georgia, asked me to go as part of an ongoing, sustained ministry there. I could never have pulled this off from scratch. But an ongoing local ministry could.

I challenge you to find a place or places to invest over a longer period than a single trip. Take students back year after year. Let them see the fruit. Help them see mission is a lifestyle, not a brief excursion. What if eventually you took students to serve where a student from your ministry now serves as the lead missionary there?

It has become far too easy in the Western church, driven by consumer values and event orientation, to do all sorts of things that are not bad in themselves yet have no sustainability. So, as with anything you do, resist the tendency of making this a self-standing trip. I have seen some churches go on mission trips that had no connection whatsoever to their local church and its mission. When external mission trips are undertaken as a part of the larger mission of the church, the long term impact is greater.

When I took a team to Cape Town in 2011, we got together and did some evangelism as a team the week before we left. I wanted to remind them that what we do there is what we also do here. Involve the whole student ministry, and in fact the whole church, in praying for and supporting the team. And when returning, help those who went to live out their lives here as they did there.

**Use short-term trips to create a long-term missional vision.** Some criticize short-term mission trips as not worth the time, energy, and money. I disagree. Such trips allow students an opportunity for immersion: They go into another culture and for the span of the trip function as full-time missionaries without the distractions of everyday life. They learn about other cultures from career missionaries. They experience ministry in a way you cannot teach in a classroom or show on a video. Biblical truth is reinforced as they see the same need for and power of Christ at work in other contexts. Students gain confidence as they serve, using their gifts and talents on the trip. And, with proper leadership, these trips can help transition students into a more missional focus after they return.

I know a student pastor named Joe who has done a great job of this. Here are a couple of stories from his students.

## Ashleigh's Story

This summer Pastor Joe told me of plans to take a group to Thailand next summer. I always had a heart for missions and had been on a few mission trips but never an international trip. Right then I had made up my mind that I would have to go on this trip! When I told my parents about the idea they were totally against the whole thing. We attended an interest meeting but my parents remained opposed. My mom was worried about the financial burden of the trip while my dad was worried about my safety. I offered to give up my birthday and Christmas presents so that I could go on the trip, but still my parents said no. At this point I just stopped trying to convince my parents to go and just sat back. I still felt a small tug on my heart to go on this trip but I did not understand why there were so many walls stopping me from going.

I came to realize that I was praying to God about the trip, but I did not trust Him concerning my parents. I started to pray that God would do the convicting. One day soon after, my mom came to me in tears saying how she knew I was supposed to go on this trip, that she felt that God was telling her that I had a heart for missions. A few weeks later my dad, also my Sunday school teacher, taught from Matthew 28 about how we should go to the ends of the earth to share the gospel. I was sitting directly in front of him that day while he stated that we, the students, should share God's Word. As he taught, tears ran down my face.

The next day when I got home from school, I sat down and wrote my dad a letter. I told him my feelings and why I felt so deeply about going to Thailand. Later that night, I taped the letter to the steering wheel of his car for him to see. When he got home from work he said we could start the process of going. We began to write letters, save money, get a passport, and complete other vital steps in international missions. I am so grateful for God's provision to let me go to the nations!

## Margo's Story

The summer after my junior year of high school, I went on a mission trip with my church to New Orleans, Louisiana. On the trip we went into homes ruined by Hurricane Katrina and worked to restore them for their owners. These people were so thankful to see what we were doing, but one thing we wanted them to know: We were there because we serve an amazing God who loves them more than they could ever imagine. Then my youth pastor informed the youth group that next year our mission trip would be to Thailand. As I saw my friends immediately get excited to serve, I sat back. I've never been one for getting out of my comfort zone. I am outgoing, but an overseas mission was something that "someone else" could go and do.

In January of 2012, I watched the Passion Conference online. Louie Giglio and Passion 2012 focused on slavery around the world. This is where my comfortable and mundane life was shattered by the fact that there are approximately 27 million slaves today. How could I sit back and watch others do the mission God has put me on? I began praying about Thailand.

As soon as I made mention of this desire, my family resisted the idea. I continued to pray. I struggled for many weeks as to whether God was calling me to go to Thailand or whether it was my own selfish desire. I definitely wanted to honor my parents. One night I realized something. What if I was supposed to be involved in the trip, but in a different way? I decided since I wasn't going to be able to go to Thailand myself, instead of pouting about it, I wanted to help another person to go and spread the gospel.

Right now I am in the process of raising nearly $3,000 for someone else to go to Thailand, and I can't wait to see what God has in store for someone.

These two young ladies from the same youth group are taking different approaches to the trip to Thailand. Both sought to honor the

Lord and the families He put in authority over them. Both have a heart for the nations, thanks in no small part to a student pastor who has led well in this process. Both glorify God.

## REACH THE CITIES, THE WESTERN "WINDOW"

One of the major emphases of global missions today is the 10/40 window.[2] In 1974, Ralph Winter presented an address at the Lausanne Congress on World Evangelization entitled "The Highest Priority— Cross-Cultural Evangelism." Winter's speech began a movement of identifying various people groups globally. This process led to a realization: Most of the unreached groups live in a large area in the East. Luis Bush coined the term the "10/40 window" in 1990 because of the longitude and latitude defining the region with the majority of unreached peoples. From then until now awareness of this region's lack of the gospel has shaped much of missions strategy. For instance, 97 percent of the population in the fifty-five most unreached countries lives in the 10/40 window.

Yet the United States of America has become the fourth-largest lost nation on earth. We certainly have far more gospel exposure than those who live in the 10/40 window, but the gospel is known in increasingly smaller numbers here. This is especially true in the large cities. The time has come for a Western version of the 10/40 window. Whereas the 10/40 window refers to the area demonstrating the greatest cause for urgency, the window to which I refer holds much promise as it manifests great need. I am referring to a revolutionary call to reach the great cities of the West and of the world.

Why cities? Some students are not ready to go overseas; others have families not ready to let them. But the melting pot of America offers countless *opportunities* for cross-cultural experiences since the nations have moved to our cities. Cities like New York, Chicago, and Miami form the center of culture and commerce for entire regions. For instance, the forty largest cities on earth hold 18 percent of the world's population but produce two-thirds of the economic output for the entire world.[3] The influence is hard to overestimate.

Outreach to cities is *biblical*. The book of Acts demonstrates that the gospel spread across the Roman world through cities. According to Wayne Meeks, "Within a decade of the crucifixion of Jesus, the village culture of Palestine had been left far behind, and the Greco-Roman city became the dominant environment of the Christian movement."[4]

Outreach to cities is *strategic* for reaching a nation. Economic, political, and cultural influence flows from cities like water streaming from a mountaintop. A major city like New York City or Chicago has more power than the state government. I would argue that if we as believers in the U.S. focused tremendous resources and emphasis on major cities such as New York, Washington, Boston, Chicago, and Los Angeles, we could change the nation.

The globalization of the world has caused cities to be more alike than different. On the surface, cities around the world have more in common with one another than with rural areas in their own nation. The massive shopping mall in Cape Town, the largest in the southern hemisphere, looked remarkably like the one we frequent in North Raleigh, for instance (except it was bigger). The same is true for the mall I recently visited in Kiev.

Pop culture, reflecting the values of the moment, changes little over space but greatly over time. I remember years ago going to London and finding one McDonald's in the whole city, but now they are everywhere. I have enjoyed Starbucks coffee all over the world. With communication and the digital world, pop culture has increased in influence. Traditional culture, which changes gradually over time but varies significantly over space, has lessened in influence in the cities. We may gain insight on reaching Warsaw and Tokyo as much by studying New York as we do by studying farmers in Poland and Japan.

We should continue to press for more students to go to the nations, while at the same time encouraging them to consider planting their lives in a great city. This weekend I was in Boston, and my host was one of our grads who is planting a church there. If we continue to instill a missional vision in our students for the cities, more could end up living and serving there. As students think about college, career, and life in general, remind them of the cities. Take students on mission trips into the heart of cities, and if you live in or near one, regularly take your students there as well.

An urgent call to the nations and to cities can have a serendipitous effect: Because people from virtually every tribe and tongue live in or are somehow connected to the great cities of the West, students who do not feel a call internationally can still interact with the nations by living in the city. Perhaps it is time to think about a Western window, playing off the 10/40 concept, which should still receive priority. In *Two Cities, Two Loves*, James Boice surmises that if only 10 percent of evangelicals in the U.S. moved to our largest cities and lived biblical lives of love, truth, and service, the entire culture would be changed.[5]

▶ Wherever you are, advance the gospel, live on mission, and make disciples as you go.

## THE NEW MISSION FIELD OF SOCIAL MEDIA

One of the most fundamental shifts in the modern world came with the printing press and the ability to mass-produce messages. The fact that the Renaissance and Reformation came during the time of the printing press is not incidental. Changes in transportation have also made an impact in the spread of the gospel. If you were to ask someone to make a map of a region some two hundred years ago, for instance, there would not be a lot of roads. Rivers would be the focus of the map, for water provided the major means of transporting goods for millennia. But along came the railroad and the automobile, and now roads form the centerpiece of our lives. These fundamental changes in transportation offered more than ease of travel; they created a new means for information to spread, not unlike the telegraph and the telephone. In each example, the gospel spread more effectively via the various means of information transfer.

And then along came the Internet. Students today live in one of the most dramatic shifts in history. The Internet has changed the world in such profound ways that we are still trying to figure out the effects. Our daughter had a hard time getting her head around the reality that her mom and I could not keep in constant contact via texting like she can today. Our son laughs at the notion of our owning something as primitive as a VCR (google it), and that technology even came years after we were married.

The world has changed. No, we have not arrived at Hanna-Barbera's cartoon predictions of personal vehicles flying through space, but fifty years after *The Jetsons*, we actually can video chat with people all over the planet.

Thomas Friedman notes three eras of globalization to illustrate the radical changes in our world today driven by the Internet.[6] Globalization 1.0 (1492–1800) focused on nations and power, with examples like the Reformation. This shrank the world from a large playing field to medium.

Globalization 2.0 (1800–2000) shifted to multinational companies accompanied by the rise of the Industrial Revolution. The world moved from medium to small. This was the shift that led to the factory mindset in churches discussed earlier. While Friedman emphasized economic and business factors, I should note here that this was also the period of great missions expansion globally.

Globalization 3.0 (2000 to now) moved from a small to a tiny playing field. In world 1.0 countries globalized, in world 2.0 companies (and I would add denominations and parachurch ministries) globalized, and in world 3.0 individuals now globalize.

The ease and speed of personal interaction is transforming our world. Cultural influence has decentralized. Social media is here to stay, although it is constantly changing. A few years ago, I told students as I traveled that MySpace would soon be replaced by Facebook. In 2007, students who heard me say that shook their heads, arguing that Facebook was only for college students. Not anymore. Now Twitter has become a dominant force in culture (what news anchors don't include their @fill-in-the-blank?). Google Plus is here as well, not to mention a myriad of others. A study by Ball State University found that among fifteen- to seventeen-year-olds, 70 percent used texting and 76 percent social media sites.[7] This will only increase in the days to come.

Social media did what even the massive search engines could not do: supplant porn as the most popular activity on the Web.[8] Twitter has become a fundamental part of ministry for me. I cannot say how many tell me I mentor them via Twitter, although the word *mentor* may be a stretch. Twitter can be very narcissistic and self-serving, but it can also provide a vital link in communication, encouragement, discipleship, and evangelism. I have met many wonderful new friends in ministry through Twitter, and I would most likely never have interacted with them otherwise. Yes, some waste their time on social media, less disciplined students in particular. But if you think social media in general is a waste of time, you do not understand the medium.

One of the experts on social media, Erik Qualman, is a man I got to know via Twitter. His helpful book *Socialnomics* (not to mention his series of "Social Media Revolution" videos on YouTube) explains the importance of social media today. He gives a telling illustration from the world of politics, noting how President Obama was light-years ahead of John McCain in leveraging social media during the 2008 election campaign. But the specific example to which I refer involves vice presidential candidate Sarah Palin. Perhaps you recall Tina Fey's truly remarkable performance as Palin on *Saturday Night Live* (*SNL*). Some argue her parodies became more newsworthy than the actual candidate. Qualman notes that the most popular was the premier sketch. NBC estimated over 50 million people watched the video clip, over half of whom watched online. Viewers of *SNL* increased over 50 percent from the year before.[9]

Because students understand social media in particular and the

Internet in general better than their parents, information once reserved for experts or libraries is now literally at their fingertips with smartphones. Students have power today like never before. Information no longer comes to the masses from specialized authority figures. We still need teachers and education, but the world has forever and fundamentally changed. A student can find the capital of a country on Google faster than she can memorize it. We can leverage this for the good of the gospel.

The Internet also makes geographical barriers far less ominous than in the past. For instance, before students travel with me internationally, they are able to discover volumes of information about our destination online. Seminary students gain invaluable and unprecedented insight when a colleague Skypes with active missionaries on the field during class. I also Skype with missional and student ministry leaders in my classes.

Friedman notes ten "flatteners" that have changed the world due to the power of the Internet. Included in this list is the collapse of the Berlin Wall in 1989, opening the way for a global world, including the euro for commerce; and the development of the Microsoft Windows platform, opening the Internet doorway around the same time. When Netscape went public, global communication became accessible to all, making Bangalore, India, a major hub for call centers. Friedman calls the resulting browser technology "one of the most important innovations in modern history."[10] Workflow software, open sourcing, and outsourcing all contribute to enabling your average joe to have more influence. Apache, the platform used by most computers in the world today, was developed by a bunch of young computer geeks and is free for all. All this led to the rise of everything from Craigslist to Wikipedia, free resources that are changing the world economically as well. Friedman describes others, including offshoring, supply chaining, and insourcing. But for our discussion his final examples offer the most helpful information.

Informing—which includes the rise of Google, Yahoo, and other search engines—has truly changed the way we live. Do you ever go a whole day without consulting Google? I rarely do. Google is the complete equalizer, shrinking the gap from expert to ordinary individual. "It is the antithesis of being told or taught," Friedman argues, adding, "It is about self-empowerment; it is empowering individuals to do what they think best with the information they want."[11] He notes radio and television offered information from one source to many. Telephone offers one-to-one information. But a search engine allows the connection to a myriad of resources and people. This provides great power to students, but also great opportunity for harm, as naive students easily fall prey to sexual or other predatory behavior online.

Friedman also notes what he calls "steroids,"[12] such as smartphones, although technology has ramped up dramatically since his book was published. As I type this, I'm sitting at a Starbucks in Raleigh, typing on my MacBook while listening to Pandora free Internet radio streaming to my iPhone. Who needs an office?

Rodney Stark observes in *The Rise of Christianity* how social networks played a vital role in the spread of the gospel in the early church. Social networks can hardly be considered new, only social networking via the Internet. Because students spend so much time updating Facebook, tweeting pictures, and googling who knows what, why not use this tool as a way to build a missional posture in their lives and a gospel-centered culture in your church? Here is a simple suggestion about how to start this.

## REACHING ONLINE COMMUNITY

I have mentioned mission trips to nations, cities, and your community. What about the online communities we all know? What if you led your students to set aside a week at the beginning of the school year as a mission trip to the world of social media? And following that experience, what if you encouraged students to use this vital tool for the gospel?

In Acts 19:8-10 we read about Paul's mission trip to Ephesus. When he arrived he did what he normally did—as a Jew, he went to the synagogue and preached Jesus. But after three months most Jews had had enough and began to, well, be difficult. So, what did Paul do? He moved to a secular place, the school of Tyrannus, and focused on teaching the gospel daily. Paul never changed the message. But he did change his approach as other opportunities came available. The Internet is such an opportunity today.

Paul used the normal networks of his day: the marketplace, the synagogue, a lecture hall. We see similar tactics in history. Martin Luther nailed his Ninety-Five Theses on the church door in Wittenberg because that was an established form of social networking. John Wesley took the practice of society meetings for all sorts of subjects and created the societies that formed the heart of the growing awakening in his day. He simply used the social networks of his time. And so should we.

In recent years we have moved from the rotary phone (yes, I remember those) to the smartphone, from snail mail to e-mail, from vinyl to iTunes, from live television to DVR, from movie theaters to Netflix. The digital world has not eliminated all the old technologies, but it has created new opportunities.

Online, students can share Jesus:

- Glocally (globally and locally)
- Directly (many students are more bold typing online than face-to-face)
- Creatively (utilizing resources like viewthestory.com and iamsecond.com)
- Interactively (involving others, leaders, websites, YouTube)

Here are a few ways you can encourage students to share, although I bet you can get with them and come up with creative ideas of your own.

- Post their testimony as a Facebook note or on their blog or Tumblr, and link to that with Twitter or status updates. Or, send a message to friends and ask them to read it and give their feedback.
- Tweet or post key verses, maybe a series noting the narrative of the gospel.
- Set aside an hour a week online just for the gospel, like "virtual visitation" where they take that time to talk to a friend about Christ.

This offers a fantastic opportunity for your students to be creative in their witness. Prestonwood Baptist Church in the Dallas-Fort Worth area recently held a campaign called the Facebook Challenge. They asked each student to record a two- to three-minute testimony video and send it to all their friends on Facebook. Student pastor Chris Lovell developed the four-week campaign, which resulted in a great involvement from students in sharing the gospel.

But as in all opportunities like this, a warning should accompany the effort. First, students cannot turn on their love for Jesus suddenly. Their whole lives (and their online profiles) should reflect a love for Christ. Second, students must be aware that their efforts will be welcomed by many but not by all. Some will criticize them, so help them go about their witness with eyes wide open. Remind them the purpose is not to debate or argue but to share good news. Most online arguments get nowhere. Remind them of the need for an accountability partner. You would never send out a student alone to go into a neighborhood to share Christ; neither should you encourage him to go online alone.

I do not want to focus here on listing all of the evils of the Internet, but make no mistake, social media has brought with it more than its share of evil, from sexting in middle school all the way to young people who have been raped and even murdered because of naïveté online. Here are a few recommendations for Internet safety:

- This is where teaching a gospel-centered life matters. Truth is, if your child wants to, he will find a way to be involved online in ways that are harmful.
- Monitor your children on their phones and online. If you have children, remember you are the parent. You have the right and in fact the responsibility to protect them. Check their texts. Have their password on all social media sites. Use Internet filters when they are young and an accountability tool such as Covenant Eyes when they get older (not just on the home computer, but especially on their phones). Remind them regularly that the wisdom they use regarding strangers offline applies to behavior online.
- Talk to your children regularly about these matters. Know your child enough to pick up signs of inappropriate activity.
- Show them how they can use the Internet in positive ways, like those described on the previous page.

We live in a radically changing time. Let us not be afraid to greet the challenges of our day with a timeless gospel. It could be that the very social media that fills the lives of students today may provide an avenue for spiritual movements. If Osama bin Laden knew how to use social media to spread his poison of terrorism, we can use it to herald the good news.

## REVIEW AND APPLICATION

- How many students do you know who have been overseas on a mission trip? How can such trips help foster a missional mindset throughout your student ministry?
- Do you have specific ways and perhaps an annual time in which you invest in your community to bring hope through ministering the gospel?

- How involved are your students in social media? How can you maximize their witness there?
- Read Matthew 28:19-20. Notice the passage says "all nations," a fundamental part of the Great Commission. How has this passage shaped your understanding of outreach?

# CHAPTER 9

# MISSIONAL VOICE

### Albany, New York

November 18, 2011. Students came in droves, mostly female, all more than excited. Many wore T-shirts in recognition of the event. Some waited in line for eleven hours. Two hours before midnight, lines filled with young adults stretched around the complex as they awaited entrance. Many brought blankets; some played board games. They talked incessantly about that for which they had waited diligently.

They were sharing good news with one another. And for weeks after, they would share their story of that night with all who would listen. These young evangelists were unashamed in their zeal.

What was the focus of their message? A movie. That night, *Breaking Dawn, Part 1* from the Twilight series opened in Albany theaters at midnight.

I'm not endorsing the movie; I'm just making a point. We do not need to help students become evangelists. They have no problem talking about a subject for which they are passionate: the latest fashion, the newest video game, their favorite sports team, the most recent viral video, you name it. If they care about it, students will talk about it. Sit in a local public school cafeteria at lunchtime and just soak in the chatter to see what I mean. Students will raise their voices and speak their minds about things they really care about.

But if it matters little to them, it will be discussed little. Or if they think the subject matter only relates to a given place like a church building or the youth group, they will save it for there. But I have seen students become passionate about sharing Christ. And when they do, it is hard to get them to stop. I tell student pastors how talking about their own witness and showing students how the gospel matters in their own lives will do more to get their students to witness than any program. When we vocalize our love for Christ, others will follow suit.

Glenn served as a student pastor while in seminary. He led his students to do a free car wash, a simple example of servant evangelism where they washed cars for free and shared Christ as they had opportunity. Acts of kindness like this open up all kinds of opportunities to share. Glenn's students watched him lead a man to Christ that day. Soon after, Glenn told me his students suddenly seemed to have a great passion for talking about Jesus simply because of his example.

This is why helping students grasp the greatness and the wonder and the glory of the Story of Christ and how that Story relates to everyday life matters more than anything you do in student ministry. When students are truly passionate about something, they will talk about it, naturally and enthusiastically engaging others.

## STUDENTS RAISE THEIR VOICES ABOUT WHAT THEY CARE ABOUT

One of the most historic and delightful Southern towns you will ever visit is Charleston, South Carolina. On my first visit to Charleston, the heritage, charm, and beauty gripped me. If you want a sense of early America, you must visit Charleston.

I visited to speak at a church where one of my students served as pastor. The young pastor earnestly sought to help his small congregation make Jesus famous in their community. On Sunday night, I did a little exercise I have done often in churches. I told them the three things people can tell about us when we get to know them, and all three relate to sharing Christ. First, they can tell if we *care* about them. People do not care how much you know about God until they know how much you care about them. Helping a neighbor with yard work, showing patience in a long line at the store, offering a kind word at the bank — the little things we do help or hinder our witness. Second, people can tell if we *believe* what we talk about. This is why we must help students grasp what the gospel message is, from Creation to Fall to Rescue to Restoration, in all its life-changing power. Finally, people can tell if the *hand of God* is on our lives. When people see we have conviction about the truth we share, that we care about them, and that something real has happened to us, our witness is multiplied in impact.

Based on this basic trilogy I offered a simple exercise. I had gospel tracts that clearly explained the gospel placed across the front of the church. I challenged the congregation to take a booklet if by so doing they were signifying a willingness to share it with another person in the next seven days. No sticking them on a car windshield, but to be used as a tool to help in conversation.

The majority of people responded to the challenge. They always do, in my experience. More believers want to serve Jesus than we think; they often need encouragement and practical guidance. But when they understand the wonder and the glory of the Story, they want to tell others.

In this little example I am not suggesting that to be missional means gathering a group of believers to tract-bomb an area. But I believe gospel booklets can still be helpful in communicating Christ to others. That night several students in their small youth group took the challenge. This was before the days of tweeting, posting, or pinning; AOL Instant Messenger and e-mail were all the rage. That week I received updates from enthusiastic students excited to realize that God could use them, as young people, in the work of the gospel.

One high school girl e-mailed me about her friend whom I will call Mark. Mark had been antagonistic to the gospel, so she wrote me asking for advice. I sent her a long e-mail explaining how to talk to her friend Mark. She forwarded the e-mail to Mark. This was not my intention when I sent the e-mail! She wrote me late the next night, elated to tell me the news that she had led Mark to Christ via IM earlier that evening! It seems that her concern for her friend, even to the point of writing some professor in another state about how to talk to him, softened his heart.

That week this handful of students led five of their friends to Christ. One of those five died unexpectedly two weeks later. Missional means far more than getting people to take a tract to a friend. But it does not involve less than sharing Christ personally either.

Don't tell me you seek to be missional or lead a missional ministry if sharing Christ personally is unimportant. If your understanding of gospel centrality does not give you a broken heart for your neighbor and the nations, I wonder what gospel you are following. The gospel led Paul to reason in the marketplace and stand in the synagogues and before rulers to share the good news. It will do the same for us.

## THEN AND NOW, JERUSALEM AND ATHENS

Personal evangelism a generation ago involved a more simple explanation of propositions than today. Around 1970, an explosion of evangelism training methods came on the scene of evangelicalism.

I am grateful to God for practical evangelistic methods and tools. I have led more than a few to Christ using them. But just because a tool is effective with some does not mean it is always the best approach for many. Generalizing the particular must be avoided in a complex world. Our world has changed, and while the gospel never changes, most people today have no background in the Scriptures. We cannot assume they know who Jesus is, or at least the Jesus clearly proclaimed in Scripture.

In Acts 2, we read of the first witnesses beginning the work of fulfilling the Great Commission. All the believers shared Christ, not just Peter (see verses 10-11). Peter only preached after all had been telling the mighty works of God. But we understand the content of their message by reading his sermon and the sermons in the early chapters of Acts, including the message of Stephen in Acts 7. In Jerusalem, facing an audience of Jews and some Gentile God-fearers with knowledge of Judaism, the early believers began their witness by proclaiming Jesus as the Messiah. This was the focus of their proclamation.

But when you get to Acts 17 you will find Paul a long way from Jerusalem and speaking to a very different group, Gentiles. When he stood at the Areopagus to share Christ, Paul made no mention of a Messiah, for these Greeks did not seek one. Instead, he started with Creation, appealed to their logic, and then went on to proclaim Christ, the resurrection, and the coming judgment, calling them to repent as Peter had in Acts 2.

What you see are the elements of the biblical narrative: Creation (verses 24-28), Fall (29-30), Rescue (30-31), and Restoration (31-32).

We once lived in Jerusalem. We now live in Athens.

A generation ago, far more people understood the basic tenets of Scripture. They had some awareness of the overarching narrative of the Bible. Not so today. When Tim Tebow painted John 3:16 beneath his eyes during the national championship game while at the University of Florida, the reference was immediately the most searched item on Google. Things we who grew up in church assume to be true are largely unknown to many people around us.

In other words, we need to be thinking like missionaries think and sharing like missionaries share. In this chapter I will suggest some practical ways to help students tell others about Jesus personally. Not how to "preach," but how to converse about the good news.

One more thing: In the New Testament we do not read of lengthy training courses and seminars on evangelism. They got the idea, the wonderful Story of the gospel, and they shared it naturally because it was a vital part of their lives. When your life has been transformed by the gospel, you need a little how-to, but not a lot. If we are to see a missional shift, we need a fundamental change in how we think about evangelism.

## FROM SKILLED PRESENTATION TO PERSONAL CONVERSATION

I remember the time I sang a solo at my high school. I was part of the choir, the year was 1976, and we performed a musical about America in honor of the bicentennial. I do not think I have ever been so nervous. I think that is how a student feels when he is made to do something in front of his peers when he has no confidence. When we make evangelism about a precise presentation that has to be done just right, we set students up for failure. But when we show them nothing matters more than the gospel, that the key is their Jesus and not their ability, and how the gospel changes everything, they will find conversations about the gospel to be meaningful.

I cannot emphasize this enough: Nothing you will ever do in ministering with students will matter more than showing them the wonder of the gospel. This involves so much more than information. It involves experiencing the unparalleled grace of God in Christ, seeing how the gospel affects everything in life, and truly encountering the God of all. You cannot have it both ways, Jesus being the center of your ministry and at the same time focusing on something else. We have to be honest with students and treat them as young adults, telling them that as we invest in the brokenness of a lost world, things will not always turn out as we would hope. We won't win every person we seek, but we will win some. We cannot be a halfway witness. The minimalist, factory approach to Christianity fails in personal evangelism more than any other place, because students will not share their heart and soul with their friends if what they share is not at the center of their lives.

In other words, you and I who lead students are constantly faced with a decision: Do we believe the love and grace of God in Christ is worth everything? Kenda Creasy Dean reminds us:

Christian love is messy and risky. It is a kind of indecorous love, like the prodigal father who literally throws himself on his smelly, wayward son who returns home; an imprudent love, like that of a shepherd who leaves ninety-nine sheep in order to go search for one directionally challenged one; a spendthrift love, like the kind that makes people deny themselves and take up their crosses to follow Jesus.[1]

She notes that in the early church you could not think of believers apart from sacrificial love (see Acts 2:41-47, for instance). At their best throughout history, in times of great spiritual renewal, believers were known for caring for the poor, loving orphans, and giving their lives to mission service, and they witnessed the mighty work of God. Unfortunately, in the church today, especially among students, Dean warns, "It is not only possible to think about the church apart from the mission of God, it is now normative to do so—even for young people who call themselves Christians."[2]

> No evangelism tool or program will substitute for a passion for Christ. When students get this—as in Jonathan Edwards' day, in the Student Volunteer Movement, or the Jesus Movement—a generation is changed.

There are still plenty of people who do not follow Christ for one fundamental reason: No one has told them how. But more than simplistic gospel presentations, people need a conversation with someone they trust. This is the Starbucks generation who seek both community and reality, but they want reality given through community. Rather than believing before belonging, they are more likely to belong before they believe. So your youth rally will still lead to decisions, but do not be misled to think a rally will reach into the depths of lostness at most middle and high schools in America.

When you teach students to share their faith personally, here are a few things they need:

**They need to understand the wonder and awe of the Story of the glory of God.** You cannot rehearse enough just how life-changing this is. They need to be shown regularly how Jesus changes our relationships and our role models, our material needs and our dreams.

**They need to recognize their resources.** When we witness, we partner with the Holy Spirit. A salesperson depends on his ability to communicate; a witness depends on the Holy Spirit! We are never alone as we share Christ, for He is there. Help them see the power of the Spirit-filled life and the confidence that comes from sharing in this power. Help them pray God-sized prayers for a lost and broken world. Help them grow in their intimacy with Christ through asking Him for their friends to be saved.

**They need to see how to live this way and how to share Christ in this context.** While true about much of life, this statement is more true of evangelism than pretty much anything else: It is *caught* more than it is *taught*. The more they see you share, the more they will as well. The great Puritan Richard Baxter had it right when he said the people you lead can tell if you have been spending much time with God, for that which they gain the most from you is what is in your heart. Every week mention someone you have shared Christ with or a relationship you are forming. My students tell me that my conversations about a bartender I go fishing with help them in their practice of witnessing more than my lists they have to memorize. The same is true for you.

**Give them a tool, a basic frame of reference to explain the gospel in conversations.** But that tool should be more than a little presentation. It should boast about a great and mighty Savior and show how His good news changes everything, not just your location on Sunday morning. And it should help them move a conversation about things students talk about toward the gospel. I just finished training for The Story, the tool I always use, at a church. A student pastor later e-mailed me, telling me how he discussed the way you can see the biblical plotline in movies.

Some middle schoolers eagerly responded, sharing examples of where they recognized gospel similarities in *The Lion King*. He told them that in the same way they had that conversation with him about a movie and the gospel, they could talk with others. And they did.

**Help them avoid compartmentalizing evangelism to a set event or night of the week, or even worse, to a few "gifted" people.** Let me say this again: We overestimate the power of our words, and we underestimate the impact of our lives and the way we structure our ministries. If your ministry structure and your own life focus evangelism on the big rally or on the monthly evangelistic blitz, you are teaching by your example that our witness is a faucet we turn on and off, and that evangelism really belongs to the big preacher-guy, not a student. No, we have to remind them and ourselves that such events and personalities can be very helpful and we should do them, but they are not the end of our evangelistic ministry, merely an overflow of our daily witness. A compartmentalized witness is indicative of a compartmentalized life where Jesus is placed in the box of our choosing.

In this way we help students by reminding them that every day God can use them to nudge people. Nudge them closer to Christ or to understanding the gospel, or nudge them away. Witnessing means communicating the gospel through words and actions, but we can enhance our witness at times when we are not able to share with words. The kind deed, the compassionate response, the integrity of one's life all contribute to one's witness, although these should not replace our spoken witness.

## FROM TALKING POINTS TO PERSONAL TESTIMONIES

If you read the book of Acts and grasp the amazing rise of Christianity within its pages, you will realize that classes for training in evangelism did not exist in the early church.

What you see in Acts regularly is the testimony of the gospel's power. In Acts 4:20, while facing their first persecution, Peter and John testify how they could not help but speak of the things they had seen and heard. Two times in Acts, Paul gives his testimony of conversion (see chapters 22 and 26). YouTube offers student ministry a great opportunity to provide regular testimonies of students in your ministry and elsewhere who live the mission. Helping students know and share their own story, in particular as it fits into God's greater Story, will give them much confidence and effectiveness in their witness. Your testimony of Christ changing you and your story of sharing that with others will be vital in developing an intentional, missional witness.

Acts records how people were astonished by what they heard. In 2:43 we read "and awe came upon every soul." In 3:10 we find "they were filled with wonder and amazement at what had happened to him." A lame man healed went from begging for money to praising the Lord. In the face of the first persecution we read of the early church in 4:13: "When they saw the boldness of Peter and John . . . they were astonished. And they recognized that they had been with Jesus." The transformation of Saul the persecutor into Paul the apostle brought astonishment (see 9:21). On Paul and Barnabas's first missionary journey in 13:12, the proconsul "was astonished at the teaching of the Lord." The teaching caused the astonishment, which I find remarkable given that a man was also struck with blindness. Do we share Christ in a way that the message astonishes both believers and unbelievers?

## FROM DIVERGENT WORLDVIEWS TO COMMON GROUND

Evangelism means changing one's worldview to line up with biblical truth. Sharing Christ means sharing a new narrative, a truer story than the one people outside of Christ know. Sharing Christ is more natural, more conversational, and more effective if we start with the other person's worldview and help him see the gospel there, and then move the focus to a biblical worldview. This is what Paul did at Mars Hill in Acts 17. He started by talking about the unknown god idol in Athens, and about truth they all pretty much affirmed: that there was a Creator and that some sense of right and wrong was obvious.

Helping students think like missionaries means they do more than just replay to others a verbal presentation. Paul said the gospel did not come to the Thessalonians only in word (although it did, and we must speak the gospel), but also in power, in the Spirit, with conviction, and through the lives they lived among the citizens there (see 1 Thessalonians 1:5). Jesus did not simply try to get people to pray a prayer but to understand and become part of a whole new kingdom. We need to help students see God at work in many ways in the world, and as we do, take a common topic and move it to a gospel conversation.

I have mentioned the world of movies and their story lines previously. Movies produced by a very nonevangelical-focused Hollywood nevertheless tell the biblical story line in one hit movie after another: Great novels (and not-so-great novels) do the same. Think about Dorothy chasing Toto in Kansas, Frodo chilling in the Shire, and things nice and calm in Gotham City. Then something goes wrong—the Wicked Witch comes along, Sauron arises, the Joker or another villain spoils the party in Gotham. Something that requires a hero, a rescuer, some sort of redemption takes place. Dorothy throws water on the witch, Frodo begins to take the ring back, or Batman returns.

These stories we love inevitably end "and they all lived happily ever after." We love stories with happy endings. Movies that endure, even in Hollywood with virtually no godly influence, have happy endings. Why do we want happy endings? Why do people want their lives to matter? This question can help introduce the Gospel Story to show the true and greater ending all want and can have.

Help students link the Story of the gospel with the brokenness in our world. I love to talk about Creation and the wonder of the natural world, then talk about how something has gone badly wrong. Seeing how a loving Jesus pushes us to care for the broken, from victims of human trafficking to lonely seniors at a nursing home, helps students take the good news from a presentation to a lifestyle. "The bottom line is this," Gabe Lyons argues. "The next wave of Christian engagement seems inherently linked to this idea of restoration. The people who are shaping this movement believe with all their hearts that God is in the restoration business—not just in the afterlife, but here on earth as well."[3]

My friends at Christ Fellowship Church in Miami have used their downtown campus, a renovated older building with more space than they can currently use, as an art center. In a part of Miami where rent is steep, the church has made a section of their facility into a free space for artists living in the area. It has created a space where conversations about art and beauty flourish, ultimately leading to conversations about the Creator who gave us the idea of beauty in the first place.

## FROM TECHNICAL SPECIALISTS TO SIMPLE STORYTELLERS

Evangelist Billy Graham has preached the gospel to more people than anyone in history. Best known for his massive crusades in major cities, what many do not know is Graham's acumen and wisdom, which have gained him favor with more than a half dozen presidents of the United States. Recently Graham was asked if he thought the Spirit was at work today in large arenas with the same effect as in his earlier days. He observed a change. "I see evidence that the Holy Spirit is working in a new way," Graham told Gabe Lyons. "He's moving through people where they work and through one-on-one relationships to accomplish great things. They are demonstrating God's love to those around them, not just with words, but in deed."[4] I believe he is right. The Internet has given individuals more influence than ever, and students are poised to leverage that influence for the good of the gospel.

But students also like to be the "expert." If you work with students you know "that guy." That guy, usually a high school student, loves to argue. That guy loves apologetics, loves to show his knowledge, and especially enjoys talking about the times he put some sinner in his place by showing his superior intellect. Apologetics matters today, but if the hero of evangelism in your student ministry is that guy, you have at least two problems: (1) Jesus was not that guy. Read the Gospels. Jesus told stories far more often than He argued. (2) Most of your students (thankfully) are not that guy and will never be that guy. Holding him up as the example of witnessing is neither most effective nor transferable. But all students love stories. Why not help them do what they already love, but give it a gospel focus?

Helping students to effectively share the Gospel Story will mean they understand the fundamental truths or propositions of the message. But it means they share it as a Story, and thus can adapt the changeless Story to a variety of contexts. Just like Jesus. Jesus adapted His message depending on the audience. At times He spoke directly; other times He used an object or example. He showed compassion and patience with the broken (woman at the well, lepers, and demoniacs), yet He confronted the self-righteous religious crowd (rich young ruler, Nicodemus, the Pharisees). In the more than forty personal encounters we read of Jesus with others, we see that even our Lord did not convert everyone with whom He shared. But we can learn from at least three ways Jesus related to others.

First, Jesus *sought* others. In Luke 19, we read how Jesus sought a hated tax collector named Zacchaeus. He intentionally sought him and ate at the tax collector's house. He met Zacchaeus where he was (verse 5), in this case sitting in a tree. He identified with a sinner regardless of the consequences (verse 7). Finally, this account shows us Jesus did not just meet sinners, He sought to save them (verses 9-10). Who like Zacchaeus, an ostracized sinner in your community, do you currently seek for the cause of Christ? Do you have names of people for whom you are praying, people with whom you are establishing friendships who do not know Christ?

Jesus was *approachable*. In John 3, we read how Nicodemus approached Jesus one night (I call that Nic at Night). Nicodemus searched for truth beyond his religious commitments (verse 2). Jesus confronted him directly (verse 3). Are you approachable? If a lost neighbor, family member, or coworker suddenly began to think of spiritual things, would they think of you as the person to speak with about their questions? Do students naturally come to you to talk about things that matter?

Third, Jesus *seized opportunities*.[5] Consider His encounter with the Samaritan woman in John 4 as He sat wearily by a well. Compare His discussion with this broken and ostracized woman to the way he spoke to Nicodemus in John 3. He approached the woman of Samaria with great care and kindness, despite her failure and sin. Married and divorced five times and currently living with a man, Jesus nevertheless spoke to her in a way that led her to embrace His truth. A simple and practical way I help students see this is through DNow weekends. When I do a DNow, we always have the students spend Saturday afternoon serving people and sharing Christ. We model in an afternoon how to seize opportunities as they come about through simple acts of service.

Help students see how Jesus and others in Scripture communicated the gospel. Champion those students who live missional lives; encourage them. More than you might expect are ready to live out the gospel with others. I had a fifteen-year-old guy talk to me at a youth camp. He told me he had—on his own because they had no youth leader—started a service and evangelism ministry that went around the community serving people, by doing yard work, for example, and sharing Christ. I commended him for taking the initiative for something like this.

"I have a question," he said hesitantly. "What if I fail?"

I told him if he failed he would no doubt be the laughingstock of his community, a failure the rest of his life, and die alone. Okay, then I told him I was only kidding.

"If you fail," I said, "try something else. Be remarkable. Live for Christ. But until then keep doing what you are doing." This young man, like countless I have met in churches, wanted to do something significant for Christ, but lived with a greater fear of failing than a healthy fear of God.

## FROM A TASK TO COMPLETE TO A VOCATION TO LIVE

I mentioned in the previous chapter the importance of getting students involved in mission trips as a part of developing a missional culture.

Setting aside time to do this locally each year can show students how to live daily, missional lives. Our church, Richland Creek Community Church, does something called *Live. Love. Serve.* each year as a ten-day mission trip in our own community. Our students play a major part in this outreach. We paint houses, clean up neighborhoods, offer backyard Bible clubs, give free car washes, and provide a free medical clinic as part of the effort. Summit Church in our area has done something similar for many years. In fact, they have done so much good in the city of Durham, from painting public school classrooms to caring for the poor, their pastor J. D. Greear was invited to be the first Anglo speaker at the annual Martin Luther King Day in the city. Helping others as we tell them about Jesus offers students a compelling way to see the gospel in action.

As you do this local mission trip, daily remind students they can be doing some form of service, and with that speak about Jesus, in the normal course of life. Remember, while we do mission trips in part because they do make an immediate impact, your long-term purpose is to help students develop a missional lifestyle. You want them to go to college, earn that degree, and begin their career thinking about how they can use all they have, are, and do for the mission.

This involves their vocation. *Vocation* comes from a Latin word that means calling.

▶ Helping students understand that their interests, abilities, future career, and relationships all relate to the mission of God will help them see living for Christ less as a task to check off a list and more as a part of why they exist in the first place.

The next Christians, of which students are a part, "don't work at jobs; they serve in vocations," Lyons argues. "They see their occupational placement as part of God's greater mission."[6]

We have to help students grasp their basic talents, gifts, and passions, which are related to calling. I love to help people "get it." I love to encourage others to grow, and I have a passion for the church to understand the greatness of the mission of God. No wonder I teach at a seminary! But I have another student who earned a degree in seminary and now works as a missionary in a major investment firm, as his undergraduate degree is in finance. He told me he has a great ministry to a host of unsaved, wealthy Republicans!

The Naperville school district near Chicago offers an example in trusting students to step up and take responsibility for their lives. In this district, of the nineteen thousand sophomores, only 3 percent are overweight, compared to 30 percent nationally. But the students in this district are not only more fit, in 1999 their eighth graders took the Trends in International Mathematics and Science Study test, an international standards test taken by 230,000 students globally. John Ratey, in his book *Spark*, observes that in a time when students in China, Japan, and Singapore rank consistently above American students, the Naperville class ranked sixth in math and *first* in science globally.[7]

What happened in this school district? Several factors, as one reason hardly ever explains such a remarkable performance. But one stands out: The beginning of school each day in Naperville, called Zero Hour, students begin not with study hall but with a fitness class. Ratey reports the role of exercise in the lives of students, noting these students learn fitness, not sports. In other words, they learn to take responsibility for their health rather than memorizing the dimensions of a volleyball court. "The underlying philosophy is that if physical education class can be used to instruct kids how to monitor and maintain their own health and fitness," Ratey observes, "then the lessons they learn will serve them for life."[8]

Imagine that, expecting young people to be responsible for developing their own fitness goals for a lifelong trajectory. Empowered by a public school district. Sounds like raising the bar to me.

The Naperville district seeks to teach a lifestyle: "The students are developing healthy habits, skills, and a sense of fun, along with a knowledge of how their bodies work."[9] You mean you can teach young people that fun is not separate from learning responsibility? Imagine if every student ministry in America helped students do this with the Word?

The Naperville school district ranks consistently in the top ten in Illinois, even though the amount of money it spends per pupil is considerably lower than other top Illinois schools. Could it be that fitness is the most inexpensive means to raise test scores? What has happened in Naperville did not begin with a brilliant educator with a Mensa-level IQ. It started with a PE teacher who read about the growing unhealthiness of American students. Naperville students start their day by running a mile with heart rate monitors. What they discovered: Learning is significantly enhanced when preceded by exercise.

I will resist the urge at this point to talk about physical discipline as a part of discipleship; that is not my point in the illustration above. What I want to point out is that if a public school district can expect such from all their students, how much more can we expect from our students who follow Jesus when it comes to the gospel?

## REVIEW AND APPLICATION

- What would happen if all your students saw how the gospel changes everything and realized that they will never do anything greater in their life vocation than use that vocation to further the gospel?
- How can you help students develop their own plan for witness while in their teen years? How can you help families do the same (see chapter 7)?
- What would happen if you helped students who attend the same high school develop a plan to reach their school?

- In Acts 2:10-11, we read that all the believers in Jerusalem, not just Peter, shared the mighty acts of God. What can you do to help students lay a foundation for being a missional teacher, or doctor, or mom, or chiropractor, or engineer, who speaks about God in their particular world?

# CHAPTER 10

# MISSIONAL STRATEGY

### Cardiff, Wales

My first visit to Cardiff came my sophomore year in college as part of a choir tour of Great Britain. Wales is the land of song; every venue we sang at was filled to capacity. I particularly recall working with young adults in Cardiff who noted their concern about the youth in their area and the lack of any apparent strategy of the churches to reach them.

Go back almost a century to another town in Wales to New Quay, Cardiganshire, where a young pastor named Joseph Jenkins labored for the Lord in a small church. In 1903 he started a Young People's Meeting, hoping to infuse some life into an otherwise dying congregation. In January 1904 God rewarded this simple strategy by allowing him to lead a teenager named Florrie Evans to Christ. The following Sunday Jenkins asked for testimonies at the Young People's Meeting after the morning service. He asked for a response to the question, "What does Jesus mean to you?" Florrie stood and nervously testified, "If no one else will, then I must say that I do love the Lord Jesus Christ with all my heart."[1] This simple, honest testimony created an atmosphere of brokenness and confession of Christ, with many openly surrendering their lives to him.

From this gathering, the Spirit began to work in the hearts of many others, ultimately leading to a profound effect on the life of an evangelist named Seth Joshua who came to Jenkins' church. He admitted he had never seen the work of the Spirit as powerfully as he did there. From there Joshua ministered at another church where a young coal miner named Evan Roberts heard Joshua preach and offered his life totally to Christ.

Short end to a long story: God used Evan Roberts as a catalyst in a movement of revival in Wales in which more than one hundred thousand came to Christ in less than a year. A key part of that movement was a young pastor who organized a meeting for youth.

Strategy matters. But here is a principle worth remembering: The more stirring of the Spirit in the work of the gospel, the less strategy you need. So, if you are in a ministry that has little gospel fervor and virtually no sense of the Spirit's power, you need a lot more strategy, right? Perhaps . . . if your strategy is seeking the face of God and celebrating and teaching the gospel despite the deadness you see. I cannot get past the fact, however, that today's church leaders seem possessed and obsessed with the how-to, and less than passionate about the One who is greater than our strategy.

The missional shift will take time. Churches are like aircraft carriers, not Jet Skis—they need time and space to change direction. Student ministries do as well. But as a young pastor of a stagnant church, I recall spending much time on my face begging for God to move. I cannot believe that the strategies we developed and the growth we saw came apart from those tears. If all you have are a collection of how-to manuals, you have no movement; you are maintaining an institution.

But strategy does matter, and we see our God as a most strategic Lord. Praise be to God, at the heart of His strategy was Jesus Christ, the atoning Son of God. He created a beautiful world and placed us in it to worship Him. After the Fall, He unfolded a strategy to rescue us. Within God's great drama of redemption many more specific strategies emerged, but all related to the Story He was writing. He chose Abraham and thus

Israel as part of that plan. Jesus our Lord chose twelve men as central in the short-term to His long-term plan. Paul regarded cities as critical to advancing the gospel, and Joshua went to cities during the time of conquest. But if you look at the strategies we see in Scripture, most were amazingly simple, and all were lashed to the greater plan of God.

## THE WHY IS GREATER THAN THE HOW

I believe that if we get the plan of God, the meat of the Word, and live for the mission, we will discover more strategic ways to minister out of our daily lives than we will learn at a hundred conferences. Just how many church-planting conferences are there, for instance? Or student-ministry gatherings? To be sure, these can be very helpful. But we over-emphasize the importance of strategy and underemphasize the work of the Spirit. A. W. Tozer said if the Holy Spirit had left the early church, 95 percent of what they did would have failed. But if the Spirit were to leave most churches today, 95 percent of what we do would continue.[2]

Remember, Jesus' strategy to reach the whole world is summarized in one simple verse, Acts 1:8. But also remember that even this verse of strategy—to go as witnesses to Jerusalem, and Judea, and Samaria, and to the ends of the earth—was prefaced with the need for power. Without the Spirit's power we take Christ's commission to the Samaritans, for instance—people we really do not like—and we reduce His commission to a "Samaritan night" once a year to reach them.

More than ten times in Acts, we read of the early church ministering *daily*, so that seemed to be a vital part of their strategy. It is actually mentioned twice in the first summary of life in the church in Acts 2:41-47, a particularly missional passage in itself. The Spirit compels us to go to Samaria, for some of us to live in Samaria, and the same is true for other regions of the world. Strategy without a gospel focus becomes merely another factory-driven approach. But the early church gave their very lives to take the gospel to the ends of the earth.

Most books on a subject like student ministry spend about 70 to 90 percent on methodology and about 10 to 30 percent on theology and philosophy. These books offer tremendous insights and great knowledge of the work of student ministry. But we have skipped the indicative and lived in the imperative until we have lost the *why*. As my friend Jeff Lovingood has noted, we can never get past the *why* of ministry. In this book I have intentionally focused 70 to 90 percent on the why and more like 10 to 30 percent on the how.

You the reader—whether you are a student pastor, parent, student worker, or a student—have been gifted by God as a unique creation in the image of God with a specific place of service and influence, and I am far more interested in helping you think through the why and the what so that in your own walk with Christ through the context of your local church you can make specific application on the how. Remember earlier when I talked about movements? Here is the reality: If all you have is a how-to manual, you have moved from a movement to an institution. But if you have the passion and focus on a missional movement centered on the gospel, you can make the application.

I have actually been focused on strategy the entire book, however. The strategy has been to help you see the importance of helping students and their families, and thus the whole church, see the world as missionaries and live as missionaries. Ephesians 4:11-12 admonishes leaders in the church to equip the saints to do the work of the ministry. That is, to be self-feeders with lives focused on the gospel and live to see the gospel change culture through changing the lives of people by the power of the gospel. I hope you are catching a redundant trend there. We help those we lead to see the world from the biblical perspective of a Creator and Redeemer God. Lovingood says in his helpful book *Make It Last*, "A clear purpose—and working from the right perspective—motivates and inspires not only us, but the people around us."[3]

In great spiritual awakenings and in times of spiritual renewal such as missions movements and church-planting movements, the strategies that arose grew out of a recovery of the gospel in its greatness. We cannot offer people, either in the church or in the world, anything more than Jesus! We cannot assume this to be our driving passion; we must constantly return to it. If methodology drives your ministry, you will be a slave to the latest method or at times the latest fad. But if theology, particularly a theology rich in gospel content *and* gospel passion, serves as your core, then you will realize there are a variety of ways to "do" ministry as you go, not a one-size-fits-all.

In this final chapter I hope to help you think on the application of the ideas in this book. If you find what is written here helpful and you believe this is the direction your student ministry should go, the first thing you may want to do is to put this book in the hands of those with whom you serve. In fact, my hope is that student ministries, including leaders (adult leaders, parents, and key student leaders) will read this together and walk through the application questions to move in a more missional trajectory.

Whatever strategy you develop for students, and whatever methods you use to succeed in the strategy, student ministry will grow out of your own life as the leader. Start with your own life and the life of those who lead with you. In fact, as Lovingood says, if you invest consistently in your leaders, and if you and your leaders get the "why" or the mission—students will get it as well.

## WHAT YOU SAY

People will follow what you champion the most. If your conviction is that the gospel of Jesus Christ is at the heart of any effective ministry, then you will talk about Jesus and His kingdom more than anything else. Just this week I heard a pastor at a church stand up before the congregation and say, "Before we go any farther in this service, I want us all to focus our attention on . . ."

What do you think he said? "The Lord Jesus Christ, because we gather today to worship Him"? Nope. He said, "I want us all to focus our attention on the bulletin as we see the many opportunities to serve the Lord here."

Welcome to life in the institutional church. Now, this minister by no means intended to communicate that the activities in the bulletin mattered more than the Lord; after all, he considered the activities service to the Lord. But we do need to be careful of our focus always. If you talk mostly or with greatest affection about your upcoming events, you are event-driven. If you talk more about acting right, you are a moralist. If you talk more about yourself, you are personality-centered. If you say more about anything other than our incredible God and glorious Savior, you are telling students Jesus is not most vital. Of course you can and must emphasize the other things. But not more than Christ.

What is essential to your student ministry? If you took Jesus out of your ministry for a week or two would He be missed? What is happening in your own life and in your ministry that can only happen because Jesus rose from the dead? A biblical strategy must not lose focus on resurrection power.

If you have a weekly student worship time, what are the essential elements? Do you really have to have a game or giveaway every week? I am not arguing here to eliminate them, but if you get up and talk about those things first every week, you are speaking volumes to students. Your well-intentioned efforts to make students feel welcome may in fact be telling them the whole night is really not that big of a deal. Make sure the most important person you talk about weekly is not you, or the students, or anyone else but Jesus.

If I were the pastor mentioned on the previous page, I would have said something like this: "Welcome to worship together this week. Before we go any further, I want to ask you to focus your attention on the God who has made a way for us to gather." I would then have prayer. After that, I would mention quickly any announcements, but how I talk about them should always, without exception, make it clear Jesus matters more.

If being missional matters, you will also talk about that more — in your own life, by the testimonies of others, throughout the teaching in the student ministry. The things you talk about tell others what matters most to you.

This includes praying. If prayer matters to you, then you will pray as if it does. But you will do more — in your praying you will give attention to gospel praying, focusing on the greatness of God and the lostness of man, on sacrificial service and risk-taking faith. Do not only consider the words you say to people for God as vital, but also give attention to the words you say to God for people. As I have said throughout, though, words alone are not enough.

## THE EXAMPLE YOU SET

At this point, you may be thinking, *I thought we were going to talk about strategy — what about events? Calendar?* Hang on. We jump to the calendar too quickly and fail to understand these more vital matters. The second issue in terms of strategy has to do with how you live, the example you set.

If you are a leader in student ministry and you are not missional, and your life does not demonstrate a yearning to center all of your life on Christ, no calendar exists that will rescue your ministry. If you are not comfortable sharing your faith, change. Get help. Find a mentor. Step out in faith. Take students and learn together. As my friends at Student Leadership University like to say, the person you are becoming is based on the people you meet, the places you go, and the books you read. That starts with meeting Jesus, going to the cross, and reading the Word. Then build on that foundation. Evangelistic, gospel-centered, missional student ministries and churches are universally led by pastors with a gospel-centered mission. This cannot be emphasized enough.

The scary reality is that if you are given influence over students for a period of time, they will become like you. My students at Southeastern who spend the most time with me do emulate me. So when Paul said, "Imitate me, just as I also imitate Christ" (1 Corinthians 11:1, NKJV), he did so understanding how he needed to be like Christ. And so should you and I.

You have to be careful because you do not want to become the hero of the students you lead. Jesus Christ is the hero, period. But you are an example. And so are all those who lead with you. If you are missional but the rest of the student workers are event-driven, you will not create a missional ethos. You must give as much attention or more to developing the leaders and parents as you do the students.

In mercy ministries three areas are vital: relief, development, and social reform.[4] Most tend to focus on relief, especially in times of natural disasters. However, the greater good is done by social reform. It does not make the headlines, it does not make those involved the heroes. But the long-term impact for good is so much greater. This is the "teaching to build a well is better than giving a bottle of water" approach.

If you are committed to developing a gospel-centered, missional student ministry, you will not give your time and energy exclusively to the ministry immediately in front of you, but you will see the vital role of digging a deep foundation for long-term cultural change. The taller the skyscraper, the deeper the foundation. You may be in a ministry marked by teaching from a Moralistic Therapeutic Deism posture. Change will take time and a lot of foundation work. But those you work with probably do love the Bible and have a heart for Jesus. They simply teach the way they have been taught; they have never been shown another way. It will take time to change that.

For example, mentoring is a big deal to me. I speak to a lot of people, but I believe my greatest impact is through mentoring. I try to take young men I am mentoring with me on every driving trip, as I noted in chapter 4. That example says to student pastors where I am speaking that mentoring is so important I do it at every opportunity, including traveling to their church. I can yap all I want about mentoring, but demonstrating it speaks louder than words.

I have a plan for growing a missional culture in the Western church. It starts as a husband and a father as I seek to help our children and now their spouses to live missionally. This has been my greatest investment. I also mentor students formally and informally to instill this in those closest to me. I consider teaching classes at Southeastern to be a form of disciple making. Further, I invest in a few people in my local church, in key leaders (especially my doctoral students), and others I mentor at a distance through social media and regular contact. Beyond that, I seek to expand a missional movement by consistently focusing on the gospel and the mission of God through social media, my blog, and as I travel and speak. Oh, and by writing books like this. I am aware that from the most personal of relationships in my family, to the students I invest in, to all those God gives me in terms of influence, my example matters more than my words, although all must work together.

## HOW WE STRUCTURE MISSIONAL MINISTRY

The third factor of strategy is the most overlooked. It has to do with how we structure ministry. Get out your calendar and look at the last year. Does it demonstrate a missional focus?

Again, Jeff Lovingood, a veteran of student ministry for about three decades, helps me with this. He offers a basic template for developing an effective strategy, and the three elements I've discussed all relate to it. Here is his grid:[5]

**Come to worship.** A missional passion will never extend to the community and the daily lives of students if it is not apparent in the times students gather for worship regularly. Worship time offers the opportunity to remind students of the mission and to celebrate those who live it.

**Connect in fellowship.** Community matters to this generation much more than compartmentalization. Small groups, mentoring, and doing life together makes fertile ground for a missional movement to grow. As a young pastor I took a deacon with me every week to share Christ. We developed a deep friendship, but we also were able to allow our friendship to show our small congregation the importance of the gospel.

**Grow in discipleship.** The goal of discipleship is to "learn to grow to disciple themselves by the work of the Holy Spirit so that they can truly own their faith."[6] This includes mentors and teachers, but it also includes helping older youth invest in discipling younger youth. We lose a lot of students at age sixteen when they get their driver's license. I have seen too many students active in student ministry become bored by the later high school years as they feel they are doing the same thing in eleventh grade that they did in seventh grade. Help each student find a ministry, and as noted earlier, to develop a missional plan for their life, as a central facet of their discipleship. Structure ministry to prioritize this.

**Serve others in ministry.** This is where we really help students see in our structure if missional Christianity really matters, or if it is just something we talk about. If living as missionaries is vital to our ministry, we will give much more attention to what we do off campus, in the community, than to what we do in the church building. We will change our scorecard of success to magnify ministry to those who need Christ. Christ Fellowship in Miami does this wonderfully, but churches with far fewer students and resources do as well. Remember, this generation wants to get up and serve, not just sit and take notes. This would include specific times when the student ministry goes as a group to serve. But it also includes Sunday school classes and small groups, the student praise band, the families involved in student ministry, all involved to be regularly serving their community and their neighbors for the sake of the gospel.

**Go reach the world.** We make a serious mistake if we assume all the students will reach the world without intentionally sharing Christ. As noted earlier, telling people about Jesus demonstrates in a very clear way that we understand our role as missionaries in a lost world.

These categories can also help in developing a scorecard that is more missional than attractional, more incarnational than institutional. In chapter 1 I mentioned the need to change the scorecard. Student pastors tell me they want to change the scorecard, but the gatekeepers (pastor, deacons, elders, parents) often hinder such changes. Have you ever sat down with church leaders to discuss how you measure success, how you keep score? Perhaps going through some of the things discussed in this book could help. Here are some ideas for a more missional scorecard, using Lovingood's grid:

**Come to worship.** Attendance at the church building, including Bible study, worship, student worship, and so on, should be part of the measurement. Don't overreact to institutional Christianity by ignoring these key measurables. The book of Acts records numbers often.

**Connect in fellowship.** This starts with baptism and connection with a local body of believers and extends to include meaningful relationships. You could measure how many Titus 2 relationships you have (older men and women investing in younger men and women), the amount of involvement in small groups, and any other ways your church already enjoys fellowship together. This could also include students in groups involved in ministry in the community.

**Grow in discipleship.** This would include scoring what you teach and the content students receive throughout the year. Do the songs they sing in a year communicate a robust, gospel-centered theology? Songs are the second place they get their doctrine, after teaching/preaching in the church. Track what they are hearing Sundays, in student worship, in Bible study, and so on. Curriculum like LifeBibleStudy from NavPress will help in this.

From the student's side of scorekeeping, how many are being mentored? That is not a small value today.

**Serve others in ministry.** You can track how much you as a ministry participate in ministry to your community and the world, and how many students are involved. This would include organized ministry and individually initiated ministry. Encourage students to be involved in ministry themselves or with their friends. You could have a message board on your website or a Facebook group where students share their stories.

**Go reach the world.** How many students participate in regular evangelistic activities, go on mission trips, or frequently share their faith. Again, you can keep score to some extent with message boards or other forms of social media. Some of the scorekeeping will not be precise numbers, like the number who go to Haiti on a specific trip, but encouraging reporting via Facebook groups or other means will help. I currently serve with the young professionals ministry at my church, and the individual small-group Facebook groups give us a pretty healthy anecdotal way to track where people are in terms of ministry and sharing their faith.

A couple of years ago, I spoke at a youth camp that involved many churches from across a state. These churches all affirm the Scripture and believe the gospel is the answer for the world. It also served as a leadership camp of sorts, with most students in attendance representing the cream of the crop from the churches represented. I preached all week and spoke to the adult leaders. On Thursday afternoon I had a session with about forty students, all of whom were rising seniors in high school. I talked to them about being missional, about living out their faith in service to the hurting and telling the great Story of redemption found in Christ. They listened attentively. At the end I asked them to choose a profession to do a little "how to be missional in that vocation" application.

A bright, blonde young woman enthusiastically said she wanted to be a dentist, an orthodontist specifically. I asked her and then the group how she could be missional. They pretty much just sat there, although there was a little effort at attractional witness, such as inviting her patients to church and so on. Nothing wrong with that. But nothing more than that either.

I then told them about a dentist I heard of who, at the end of each year, discovered which patients had not paid their bills. Instead of sending a threatening letter (he was, after all, doing well in his practice), this dentist wrote each of these families a personal letter. He told them how much they owed, spelling each bill out in precise detail.

Then he wrote that the bill they owed as of the opening of the letter was forgiven. They no longer owed him. And he asked them to continue coming to his practice. He continued to write the reason for the debt being forgiven, explaining that Christ had forgiven an enormous debt he could never hope to pay on his own. He explained grace, the love of Christ, and the beauty of the gospel.

Students across the room began to light up with enthusiasm and awareness, like that aha moment one gets when discovering something wonderful. Suddenly they began to offer other suggestions in different professions. They really could figure this out once they began to see how missional became practical.

These students had grown up their entire lives in Bible-believing churches. But they had no clue how to transfer their faith from the church building to the office building, from the factory to the community. This is ministerial malpractice of some sort.

What can you and I do for students that is more important than showing them how to live out their faith?

## REVIEW AND APPLICATION

- What is your church's strategy to reach and disciple students? Can you articulate it in a couple of sentences?
- If someone asked a leader in your church's student ministry or one of your key students to describe the purpose and strategy of your student ministry, how would they respond?
- When you think of strategy do you start with the events you normally do or the gospel with which you have been entrusted?
- In Acts 1:8 Jesus lays out a simple strategy for His followers: In the Holy Spirit's power, be witnesses beginning in your local community (Jerusalem), your region (Judea and Samaria), and to the ends of the earth. How does your strategy as a student ministry compare to this?

# CONCLUSION

While in seminary, Michelle and I were actively involved in the student ministry at our local church. We taught the tenth-grade boys' class one year, and on Wednesday nights I volunteered with the student ministry while Michelle went to choir practice. Two of the other volunteers were students in seminary as well. One was Erwin McManus, a pretty well-known author and church leader who now lives in Los Angeles. The other was George Guthrie, who like me went on to earn a PhD and now teaches full time, in his case at Union University. George and I each have sons named Joshua, although mine prefers to be called Josh.

I want to conclude with the story of Joshua Guthrie, as he illustrates what I have tried to say in this book. For Joshua, Christianity can never be a factory-style show-up-and-do-as-little-as-possible experience. Here is Joshua's story, which brings together the need for both water to drink and the Water of Life:

My specific ministry is an organization called "Dollar for a Drink." For years my family supported World Vision during Christmas and I had always been interested in supporting the fresh water section of their catalogues. Unfortunately, the "big one" cost about $10,000—and I was just a fifteen-year-old guy! But then in the summer of 2008 my dad got me a special book to read: Alex and

Brett Harris's *Do Hard Things*. This book finally gave me the challenge I needed to get going on the project. Dad and I discussed what it would take and we started up the organization, obtaining official IRS non-profit status and setting up an official site.

I spread the word online and it snowballed. The organization has had a total of three "campaigns" since '08—we've raised about $50,000 for four wells in Sudan and 480 filter systems in Kenya. We work with Baptist Global Response, who installs the wells after we've done the fund-raising. My role has simply been to challenge others to give.

While providing drinking water is the platform, sharing living water is the ultimate goal here. My interest in helping the poor in need across the globe started with my parents' values, which in turn depended on the gospel. If it weren't for Christ, none of this would have happened.

Here is the question: How are you going to spend your life? Are you going to waste it away hanging out at the mall and playing video games? Now don't get me wrong: I grew up playing video games and I appreciate them. However, where will you pack your *real* punches? There's so much you can be doing with your extra time and youthful energy! Will you waste your teen years and simply do the "surface level stuff" of nominal Christianity, or will you cash your years in for stuff that lasts—both for your life and lives of countless others? God has made us for so much more. I challenge my fellow students to three things: One, while hard to "get going," this stuff actually gets pretty cool once you start to see the Lord working! He is so faithful, so step out in faith to what you feel He is calling you to do. Sure, it's hard (not gonna lie, I've had some pretty discouraging times with DfaD), but the rewards are worth it.

Secondly, JUST DO IT. Seriously, the hardest part by far is getting started. Your head is so full of doubts, but just step forward in faith. Now, be realistic (like, don't try to raise $100,000 for the homeless your first year). Think it through, be wise, but eventually do *something*.

And finally: collaboration. It makes things so much easier. Try to get several others to work with you and be a team. Not only will the work be easier, but you'll have way more fun than if you're alone.

Nothing like a Millennial to call other Millennials to join him in the mission. Why don't you and I join that movement?

# NOTES

## Introduction

1. Erik Qualman, "Over 50% of the World's Population Is Under 30 — Social Media on the Rise," Socialnomics, April 13, 2010, http://www.socialnomics.net/2010/04/13/over -50-of-the-worlds-population-is-under-30-social-media-on -the-rise.
2. "Who Is Generation We?" Generation We, accessed March 19, 2012, http://www.gen-we.com. Some say the birth years are 1982–2000.
3. Gabe Lyons, *The Next Christians: Seven Ways You Can Live the Gospel and Restore the World* (New York: Random House, 2010), Kindle edition, 5.

## Chapter 1: Missional Generation

1. Reggie McNeal, *Missional Renaissance: Changing the Scorecard for the Church* (San Francisco: Wiley, 2009), Kindle edition, 13.
2. "What Is Missional?," Missional Church Network, accessed August 17, 2012, http://missionalchurchnetwork.com/ what-is-missional.

3. Christopher Wright, *The Mission of God: Unlocking the Bible's Grand Narrative* (Downers Grove, IL: InterVarsity, 2006), 31–32.
4. "What Is Missional?"
5. Emil Brunner, *The Word and the World* (London: SCM Press, 1931), 108.
6. "What Is Missional?"
7. Alvin L. Reid, *Raising the Bar: Ministry to Youth in the New Millennium* (Grand Rapids, MI: Kregel, 2004).
8. David Balkan, "Adolescence in America: From Ideas to Social Fact," *Daedalus* 100 (1971): 979–995.
9. Kenda Creasy Dean, *Almost Christian: What the Faith of Our Teenagers Is Telling the American Church* (Oxford: Oxford University Press, 2010), Kindle edition, 8. By permission of Oxford University Press, Inc.
10. Dean, 9. By permission of Oxford University Press, Inc.
11. National Study of Youth and Religion, http://www.youthandreligion.org.
12. Christian Smith with Melinda Lundquist Denton, *Soul Searching: The Religious and Spiritual Lives of American Teenagers* (Oxford: Oxford University Press, 2009), 118, 144, 162, etc.
13. Dean, 4. By permission of Oxford University Press, Inc.
14. Dean, 6. By permission of Oxford University Press, Inc.

### Chapter 2: Missional Idea

1. Jared Wilson, *Gospel Wakefulness* (Wheaton, IL: Crossway, 2011), 19–20. Used by permission of Crossway, a publishing ministry of Good News Publishers, Wheaton, IL 60187, www.crossway.org.
2. A. Hirsch, *Forgotten Ways: Reactivating the Missional Church* (Grand Rapids, MI: Brazos Press, 2006), 27.
3. J. D. Greear, *Gospel: Rediscovering the Power That Made Christianity Revolutionary* (Nashville: Broadman, Holman, 2011), 10.
4. Gabe Lyons, *The Next Christians: Seven Ways You Can Live the*

*Gospel and Restore the World* (New York: Random House, 2010), Kindle edition, 16.

5. Kenda Creasy Dean, *Almost Christian: What the Faith of Our Teenagers Is Telling the American Church* (Oxford: Oxford University Press, 2010), Kindle edition, 16. By permission of Oxford University Press, Inc.

6. Lyons, 51.

7. Kevin Kelly, *What Technology Wants* (New York: Penguin, 2009), Kindle edition, 62.

8. Paul Tripp, *A Quest for More* (Greensboro, NC: New Growth Press, 2007), 18.

9. Theologian Peter Kreeft calls this the greatest statement ever made outside the Bible. See Peter Kreeft, "Heaven," PeterKreeft.com, http://www.peterkreeft.com/topics/heaven.htm.

10. Francis DuBose, *God Who Sends: A Fresh Quest for Biblical Mission* (Nashville: Broadman, Holman, 1983), 79.

11. Lyons, 135.

12. To learn more about missional worship, see Mark Liederbach and Alvin L. Reid, *The Convergent Church: Missional Worshipers in an Emerging Culture* (Grand Rapids, MI: Kregel, 2009).

13. Adapted from Seth Godin, *Linchpin* (New York: Penguin Books, 2010), 2.

14. Dean, 12. By permission of Oxford University Press, Inc.

### Chapter 3: Missional Movement

1. "Calvary Chapel," Wikipedia, http://en.wikipedia.org/wiki/Calvary_Chapel.

2. Alvin Reid, "First-Person: Remembering the Haystack Prayer Meeting," Baptist Press, September 22, 2006, http://www.sbcbaptistpress.org/bpnews.asp?id=24037.

3. Soong-Chan Rah, *The Next Evangelicalism: Freeing the Church from Western Cultural Captivity* (Downers Grove, IL: InterVarsity, 2009), 13.

4. See Thom S. Rainer and Jess W. Rainer, *The Millennials* (Nashville: Broadman, Holman, 2011), 7. See also Neil Howe and William Strauss, *Millennials Rising: The Next Great Generation* (New York: Vintage Books, 2000), 7.

5. Rainer and Rainer, 19.

6. Rainer and Rainer, 21.

7. Gabe Lyons, *The Next Christians: Seven Ways You Can Live the Gospel and Restore the World* (New York: Random House, 2010), Kindle edition, 47.

8. Naomi Schaefer Riley, *God on the Quad: How Religious Colleges and the Missionary Generation Are Changing America* (New York: St Martin's Press, 2005), 5–6.

9. Lauren Sandler, *Righteous: Dispatches from the Evangelical Youth Movement* (New York: Penguin Group, 2006), 5, 10.

10. Sandler, 11–12.

11. Sandler, 14.

12. Sandler, 9.

13. Timothy Keller, *Generous Justice: How God's Grace Makes Us Just* (New York: Dutton, 2010), 139.

### Chapter 4: Missional Church

1. "Industry Facts," Entertainment Software Association, accessed August 17, 2012, http://www.theesa.com/facts/index.asp.

2. For more on the impact of the factory on culture, including the church, see Seth Godin, *Tribes: We Need You to Lead Us* (New York: Penguin Group, 2008). I first began thinking of the impact of the factory on culture, including the church, through the writings of Seth Godin, in particular his book *Tribes*.

3. Lynne C. Lancaster and David Stillman, *The M-Factor: How the Millennial Generation Is Rocking the Workplace* (New York: HarperCollins, 2010), 7.

4. Jürgen Moltmann, *The Church in the Power of the Spirit*, trans. Margaret Kohl (New York: Harper and Row, 1977), 10.

5. Francis DuBose, *God Who Sends: A Fresh Quest for Biblical Mission* (Nashville: Broadman Press, 1983), 106.

6. Reggie McNeal, *Missional Renaissance: Changing the Scorecard for the Church* (San Francisco: Wiley, 2009), Kindle edition, 23.

7. Mark Driscoll, *The Radical Reformission: Reaching Out Without Selling Out* (Grand Rapids, MI: Zondervan, 2004), 20–22.

8. Kenda Creasy Dean, *Almost Christian: What the Faith of Our Teenagers Is Telling the American Church* (Oxford: Oxford University Press, 2010), Kindle edition, 24. By permission of Oxford University Press, Inc.

9. Dean, 64. By permission of Oxford University Press, Inc.

10. Dean, 23. By permission of Oxford University Press, Inc.

11. Ken Ham and Britt Breemer, *Already Gone: Why Your Kids Will Quit Church and What You Can Do to Stop It* (Green Forest, AR: Master's Books, 2009), 41.

12. Dave Kinnaman with Aly Hawkins, *You Lost Me: Why Young Christians Are Leaving Church . . . And Rethinking Faith* (Grand Rapids, MI: Baker, 2011), chapters 5–10.

13. McNeal, 10.

### Chapter 5: Missional Lens

1. Terrence McNalley, "There Are More Slaves Today Than at Any Time in Human History," AlterNet, August 24, 2009, http://www.alternet.org/world/142171/there_are_more_slaves_today_than_at_any_time_in_human_history.

2. Seth Godin, *Linchpin: Are You Indispensable?* (New York: Penguin Group, 2010), 1.

3. Godin, 4.

4. Reggie McNeal, *Missional Renaissance: Changing the Scorecard for the Church* (San Francisco: Wiley, 2009), Kindle edition, xiv.

5. Godin, 84.

6. Kevin Kelly, *What Technology Wants* (New York: Penguin Group, 2010), 244.

7. Samuel Bickersteth, "The Missionary Message of Canterbury," *International Review of Mission* 11, no. 4 (October 1922): 515.

## Chapter 6: Missional Surgery

1. Tim Keller, "Talking About Idolatry in a Postmodern Age," The Gospel Coalition, April 2007, accessed August 17, 2012, http://www.stevekmccoy.com/keller-idoaltry.pdf.
2. James K. A. Smith, *Desiring the Kingdom: Worship, Worldview, and Cultural Formation* (Grand Rapids, MI: Baker, 2009), 20.
3. Smith, 21.
4. Smith, 22.
5. Tullian Tchividjian, "Spurgeon on the Removal of Idols," The Gospel Coalition, August 6, 2009, http://thegospelcoalition.org/blogs/tullian/2009/08/06/spurgeon-on-the-removal-of-idols.
6. David Platt, *Radical: Taking Back Your Faith from the American Dream* (Colorado Springs, CO: Multnomah, 2010).
7. Dan Kimball, *They Like Jesus but Not the Church* (Grand Rapids, MI: Zondervan, 2007), 44.
8. Kyle Idleman, *Not a Fan: Becoming a Completely Committed Follower of Jesus* (Grand Rapids, MI: Zondervan, 2011), 24.
9. Kimball, 45.
10. See chapter 1 for a fuller discussion of the rise of the concept of adolescence.
11. See Alvin L. Reid, *Raising the Bar: Ministry to Youth in the New Millennium* (Grand Rapids, MI: Kregel, 2004), 58–62.
12. Terrence O. Moore, "Wimps and Barbarians: The Sons of Murphy Brown," The Claremont Institute, January 8, 2004, http://www.claremont.org/publications/crb/id.1192/article_detail.asp.
13. Moore.

## Chapter 7: Missional Families

1. Paul David Tripp, *The Age of Opportunity: A Biblical Guide to Parenting Teens* (Phillipsburg, NJ: P & R Press, 2001), 14–15.
2. Thom S. Rainer and Jess W. Rainer, *The Millennials* (Nashville: Broadman, Holman, 2010), 3.
3. Kenda Creasy Dean, *Almost Christian: What the Faith of Our Teenagers Is Telling the American Church* (Oxford: Oxford University Press, 2010), Kindle edition, 111. By permission of Oxford University Press, Inc.
4. Steve Wright, *reThink* (Wake Forest, NC: InQuest Publishing, 2007), 31.
5. Dean, 109. By permission of Oxford University Press, Inc.
6. Tripp, 116.
7. "Zac Sunderland: An Amazing Adventure," The Rebelution, April 8, 2009, http://www.therebelution.com/blog/2009/04/zac-sunderland-an-amazing-adventure. See also http://www.zacsunderland.com.
8. Kevin Kelly, *What Technology Wants* (New York: Penguin Group, 2011), 246.
9. Lynne C. Lancaster and David Stillman, *The M-Factor* (New York: HarperCollins, 2010), 7.
10. Dr. James Dobson, *Dr. Dobson Answers Your Questions* (Carol Stream, IL: Tyndale, 1988), quoted in Carol Mader, *Kids' Travel Guide to the Ten Commandments* (Loveland, CO: Group Publishing, 2001), 11.

## Chapter 8: Missional Vision

1. David Platt, *Radical Together* (Colorado Springs, CO: Multnomah, 2011), 87.
2. Some of this information comes from my book *Evangelism Handbook: Biblical, Spiritual, Intentional, Missional* (Nashville: Broadman, Holman, 2009), 439–451.

3. Kevin Kelly, *What Technology Wants* (New York: Penguin Group, 2011), 84.
4. Wayne Meeks, in Rodney Stark, *The Rise of Christianity* (New York: HarperOne, 1997), 160.
5. James Montgomery Boice, *Two Cities, Two Loves: Christian Responsibility in a Crumbling Culture* (Downers Grove, IL: InterVarsity, 1996), 165ff.
6. Thomas Friedman, *The World Is Flat: A Brief History of the Twenty-First Century* (New York: Farrar, Straus & Giroux, 2005), 9–10.
7. Erik Qualman, *Socialnomics: How Social Media Transforms the Way We Live and Do Business* (San Francisco: Wiley, 2009), 216–217.
8. Qualman, 1.
9. Qualman, 9–10.
10. Friedman, 58.
11. Friedman, 157.
12. Friedman, 157.

### Chapter 9: Missional Voice

1. Kenda Creasy Dean, *Almost Christian: What the Faith of Our Teenagers Is Telling the American Church* (Oxford: Oxford University Press, 2010), Kindle edition), 88–89. By permission of Oxford University Press, Inc.
2. Dean, 89. By permission of Oxford University Press, Inc.
3. Gabe Lyons, *The Next Christians: Seven Ways You Can Live the Gospel and Restore the World* (New York: Random House, 2010), Kindle edition, 60.
4. Lyons, 8.
5. For a more thorough discussion on this, see Alvin L. Reid, *Evangelism Handbook: Biblical, Spiritual, Intentional, Missional* (Nashville: Broadman, Holman, 2009), 62–63.
6. Lyons, 112.

7. John Ratey, *Spark: The Revolutionary New Science of Exercise and the Brain* (New York: Little, Brown, 2008), 8.
8. Ratey, 9.
9. Ratey, 12.

### Chapter 10: Missional Strategy

1. Malcolm McDow and Alvin L. Reid, *Firefall* (Nashville: Broadman, Holman, 1998), 254.
2. "Lectionary Reading: The Dimensions of the Spirit's Work," Kirk o' Field Parish Church, May 2007, http://www.kirkofield.com/NewSermons/WorkofSpirit.htm.
3. Jeff Lovingood, *Make It Last: Proven Principles for Effective Student Ministry* (Colorado Springs, CO: NavPress, 2012), 22.
4. Timothy Keller, *Generous Justice: How God's Grace Makes Us Just* (New York: Dutton, 2010), 113.
5. Summarized from Lovingood, chapter 6.
6. Lovingood, 50.

# ABOUT THE AUTHOR

ALVIN REID is a professor of evangelism and student ministry and the Bailey Smith Chair of Evangelism at Southeastern Baptist Theological Seminary. A popular speaker and prolific author on subjects including evangelism, student ministry, disciple making, and spiritual awakenings, Alvin can be reached at www.alvinreid.com. For information on ministry training, go to sebts.edu. Follow Alvin on Twitter: @alvinreid.

# OTHER BOOKS BY ALVIN L. REID

*With: A Practical Approach to Informal Mentoring.* NavPress, 2012.

*The Book of Matches.* NavPress, 2012. (with Ashley Marivittori Gorman)

*Evangelism Handbook: Biblical, Spiritual, Intentional, Missional.* Broadman & Holman, 2009.

*The Convergent Church: Missional Worshipers in an Emerging Culture.* Kregel, 2009. (with Mark Liederbach)

*Join the Movement: God Is Calling You to Change the World.* Kregel, 2007.

*Raising the Bar: Ministry to Youth in the New Millennium.* Kregel, 2004.

*Radically Unchurched: Who They Are and How to Reach Them.* Kregel, 2002.

*Introduction to Evangelism.* Broadman & Holman, 1998.

# MY LIFE IS **TOUGHER** THAN MOST **PEOPLE REALIZE.**

I TRY TO
KEEP EVERYTHING
IN BALANCE:
FRIENDS, FAMILY, WORK,
SCHOOL, AND GOD.

IT'S NOT EASY.

I KNOW WHAT MY
PARENTS BELIEVE AND
WHAT MY PASTOR SAYS.

BUT IT'S NOT
ABOUT THEM.
IT'S ABOUT ME...

ISN'T IT TIME I
OWN MY FAITH?

THROUGH THICK AND THIN, KEEP YOUR HEARTS AT ATTENTION, IN
ADORATION BEFORE CHRIST, YOUR MASTER. BE READY TO SPEAK
UP AND TELL ANYONE WHO ASKS WHY YOU'RE LIVING THE WAY
YOU ARE, AND ALWAYS WITH THE UTMOST COURTESY. 1 PETER 3:15 (MSG)

**www.navpress.com** | **1-800-366-7788**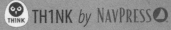